Crime and Punishment in Jewish Law

Studies in Progressive Halakhah
General Editor: **Walter Jacob,** published in association with
the Solomon B. Freehof Institute of Progressive Halakhah,
Pittsburgh and Tel Aviv

CRIME AND PUNISHMENT IN JEWISH LAW

❖ ❖ ❖

Essays and Responsa

Edited by

Walter Jacob
and
Moshe Zemer

Berghahn Books
New York • Oxford

First published in 1999 by

Berghahn Books

© 1999 Walter Jacob and Moshe Zemer

Library of Congress Cataloging-in-Publication Data
Crime and punishment in Jewish law : essays and responsa / edited by
Walter Jacob and Moshe Zemer.
    p.   cm. -- (Studies in progressive halakhah : [v. 9])
    Includes bibliographical references and index.
    ISBN 1-57181-197-4 (alk. paper)
    1. Criminal law (Jewish law)   I. Jacob, Walter, 1930– .
    II. Zemer, Moshe, 1932– .   III. Series.
    LAW   99-28244
    296.1'8--dc21   CIP

British Library Cataloguing in Publication Data
A catalogue record for this book is available from the British Library.

CONTENTS

Part 2 *Selected Reform Responsa*

Dedicated
to the memory
of
Herbert Jacob
A scholar in this field

and

Harold Ruttenberg
A true friend of the Institute

ACKNOWLEDGMENTS

We continue to be grateful to the Rodef Shalom Congregation for supporting the Freehof Institute of Progressive Halakhah and its assistance in technical matters connected with the publication of this volume. We wish to thank Barbara Bailey for her efforts with some of the typescript for this volume as well as previous volumes.

INTRODUCTION

"When the State of Israel has its share of thieves, prostitutes, and thugs, then it will be a normal state like all others" is a statement attributed to Ben Gurion; he wished to characterize Israel as a "normal" land among all other nations. Actually this should have been the least of his worries as we have always had such a criminal element in our midst.

Judaism has sought to move in the other direction and to minimize this criminal element. As a "chosen people," we would, hopefully, have a lower percentage of criminals in our midst. The aim is laudable, but the goal has never been attained. The legal systems that we have developed since Biblical days had to deal with crime and the criminal in an ethically effective way. The Bible presents only a small portion of the laws necessary for a state to function; undoubtedly criminal law developed separately as royal prerogative, although we know nothing about this. The later halakhah as we see it in the Mishnah and Talmud had to be creative even though the power of its courts both in Babylon and Palestine was limited. Whole tractates of the Talmud discuss a wide variety of legal issues both civil and criminal. Some elements of this material have been incorporated into modern Israeli law, but that is not the subject of this volume. We are concerned with the way in which the halakhic approach can shape our modern thinking in this area wherever we live, in the Diaspora or in Israel.

As we look at the halakhah, we must immediately distinguish between the practical and the purely theoretical. Although the jurisdiction of the bet din was limited in every land where we lived, the scholars felt that it was important to develop a system which dealt with every aspect of life. This meant that scholars had the luxury of discussing criminal proceedings without concern for the practical realities of human nature. They could generalize; they were able to avoid the difficult and often expensive problems of enforcement; they did not need to worry themselves over the consequences of excessive leniency. They sought an ideal solution to problems in which compromise is inevitable. On the other hand, the rabbinic scholars who had to answer specific questions which dealt with critical issues in their respective communities were forced to be practical and did not hesitate to go beyond the traditional halakhah in order to protect the community or to rid it of criminals.

This mixture of idealism and reality shape the later rabbinic discussions. The discussions are valuable for us as they present another set of insights into problems which are much debated in the contemporary world. This area of the halakhah is very broad and has been little studied. The essays and responsa of this volume explore a limited number of facets of this subject. We hope that they will stimulate further efforts.

Part One

ESSAYS

Chapter 1

❖   ❖   ❖

THE CONCEPT OF CRIME IN THE JEWISH TRADITION

Stephen M. Passamaneck

The preparation of this paper has afforded me the very welcome opportunity to re-examine some ideas, thoughts, and theories I have developed over the last twenty years. I can be very specific about the time involved, because for the past two decades I have been affiliated with law enforcement. During most of this period, I served as a chaplain with the Los Angeles County Sheriff's Department. I stepped away from those duties last year and assumed a chaplaincy for the Bureau of Alcohol, Tobacco and Firearms of the U.S. Treasury Department. In 1986, I entered the Sheriff's Academy and emerged fourteen weeks later as a sworn Reserve Deputy Sheriff.

Not surprisingly, my experience in law enforcement prompted two decades of research and study and writing in the field of law enforcement and the administration of criminal justice as reflected in the halakhah. Research grew from field experience, and field experience suggested lines of research, altogether a happy combination for me.[1]

Notes for this section begin on page 20.

I shall attempt to discuss the concept of crime from as concrete point of view as I can. For me, the subject is a very real one since I have dealt with very real crime and very real criminals. My biases, such as they are, are akin to those of a peace officer, not a criminologist, a philosopher, or a social critic; but I hope they do not show through too often.

Let us then consider the concept of crime as a living issue. What does the tradition say about serious offenses? What are they? What does our tradition reveal about a concept of crime—as though the tradition were confronted with the necessity of administering a system of criminal justice right here and right now.

In fact, let us assume that through some mysterious alchemy of time and circumstance, all of us suddenly became magistrates in criminal cases. Moreover, let us imagine that we are charged to use Jewish law in our decisions. What says Jewish jurisprudence on the concept of crime? What does it look like in the sunlight of a real world?

The first matter for our consideration is the term "crime" itself. Let us spend some time on the definition of crime because how we define something reflects how we conceptualize it. The definition is often the articulation of the concept—nothing more, nothing less. The words we use to define something subtly become what that thing really is in our minds and that definition or articulation provides the starting point for how we think of it and understand it. Thus, the idea of crime: what is it and what is it not? Crime is much more than mere anti-social behavior, though in common speech we refer to many types of misbehavior or perceived misbehavior as crimes. Conversely, it is less than ordinary anti-social behavior, since such behavior must meet specific and rigid standards before it is classified as a crime.

In the Jewish tradition the matter of crime becomes very involved indeed when we take a genuinely serious look at it and eschew rather elastic emotional views of the subject. Here is the problem: the word "crime" is not a term found in the Jewish legal tradition. It does not appear in the halakhah. The word "crime" comes from the Latin *crimen*, meaning accusation or fault, from the verb that means to render a judicial decision. From Latin and the Roman legal tradition, the word found its way into the English common law, where it is not strictly a technical term, but a rather general noun denoting a violation of the law, either human law or divine law, which violation is grievous. We shall revert to the matter of divine law presently, but for now, let us stick with human law. Even though the word "crime" is a rather general term, modern law has defined it with some precision.

A crime is a public offense; it is a violation of the peace of the State as such.[2] The notion of public offense does not of course suggest that the act in question may not occur in private. Some crimes, for instance rape and arson, are perpetuated in the most private of venues. The public part of public offense has to do with the interest of the public as a whole in it, in terms of detection, suppression, prosecution, and punishment. Whether the particular crime is a serious felony or a less weighty misdemeanor, the wrongful act constitutes more than an offense against an individual. It is in some manner an affront to society as a whole. That is why in criminal prosecution the cases are entitled with the solemn formula: the State, or the Crown, versus an in individual.

This notion of the State is crucial to the idea of crime. Indeed, the entire field of criminal justice as we know it in our day and age, and as it has developed in western history for more than a thousand years, is a first cousin to the concept of political sovereignty and political power. Without the latter, the former has no reality. A criminal justice system without the authority of the State to enforce it is not a criminal justice system. It may be high and wonderful theory, but it possesses no substance in a real world.

By contrast, we advert to the concept of civil law where the offense or wrongdoing lies between individuals or private entities, as in *Roe v. Wade* or *Smith v. Jones Lumber Co.* You are correct if you conclude that this distinction between public wrongdoing and, so to speak, private wrongdoing will continue to figure in this paper.

But what idea or concept of the State do we find in Jewish tradition? Is there some sense of the modern notion of the politically sovereign State lurking in the pages of our revelation? And if there is, does that State ever play a role in the prosecution of wrongdoers which is, after all, the heart of the matter when we speak of crime and criminal justice?

By and large, the Jewish people became a corporate entity at Mt. Sinai. There amid smoke, thunder, lightning, fear and trembling the Torah came to our ancestors through the agency of Moses the law giver. The scene at Sinai evoked profound awe to say the least; the joy and delight flowing from every word of

Torah came later. In the first stage, a terrifying covenant between the Divine and the Jews emerged, our ancestors in awestruck reverence responded to the law: "we shall do and we shall hearken."

Of course the covenant was in some sense a contract, or better yet a treaty between God and the Jews. And rabbinic tradition emphasizes that the Covenant of Torah did indeed involve the consent of the governed.[3] Yet the converse argument is also present: Torah was given under threat, under duress, with the warning—accept or perish.[4] Consent gained in this manner is clearly something less than the free volitional agreement undertaken by equals on an equal footing. Moreover, who could argue that divine power and majesty and human weakness and frailty represent a parity or equality of the parties? But let us leave this matter aside; it will only open areas of debate beyond the scope of crime and punishment. The important point here, is that the Jewish people in some sense and through some experience at the ancient mountain became one people, albeit composed of tribes that did not always live comfortably together.

The Jews in that early epoch became a sort of Religion State. They were not always religious, but their peoplehood grew from a common religion and the law of that religion. Their sovereign was God. In the course of time our ancestors rather willfully, and impertinently so it seems, chose to have flesh and blood kings as the other nations did. But even the Davidic monarchs were themselves under the ultimate sovereignty of the Divine. They enjoyed an exalted status but were not supposed to be a law unto themselves. They, too, owed allegiance to God and divine law as did the most humble of their subjects. Witness Nathan's denunciation of David in the matter of Uriah.[5]

The later Hasmonean kings were, however, excused from participation in the rabbinic legal system, but clearly they did retain the status, privileges and powers of the royal office, whatever in fact those happened to be.[6] And, too, whatever in fact did happen from day to day in the generations of the Davidic monarchs, any questions we raise regarding criminal law and the concept of crime are not resolved by any royal legal heritage we possess today. The role of monarchy will receive a closer look as we progress.

Before the kings, of course, a series of tribal chieftains, or judges so-called, exercised some leadership or governance here and there. Yet they were hardly rulers of the entire religion community, and their sovereignty if such there was, did not amount to the power of a State, even an ancient one such as Egypt or Assyria or even Philistia.

Throughout those early epochs, there was also the concurrent leadership and officialdom of the Religion State itself—the priesthood—which was certainly a locus of power and authority for our ancestors. I shall revert to this matter presently.

Let us examine for a moment, the content of the Torah, which was the focus and constitution of our ancient religious society. The redoubtable findings of biblical criticism aside, we have a body of rules and regulations that purport to be the law of our people from the time of Sinai and henceforward forever. No matter that this part was the covenant code and that part was the Holiness Code and some other part was the Deuteronomic code, Torah as a whole at some point emerged as the cornerstone of the corporate existence of the Jewish people as the servants of their God.

The Torah generally addresses its comments and warnings to individuals. Blessings and curses for fulfillment or non-fulfillment of the duties therein prescribed may fall upon the people as a whole, but the specific duties are most often addressed to individuals—Thou shalt in the singular and Thou shalt not, in the singular. Occasionally there are commands which only make sense if directed to a group—such as "Judges and officers shall you appoint for yourselves"[7]; but the laws are far more commonly couched in the singular.

Among those laws there are certain warnings about the eventual establishment of a monarchy, and these are doubtless pointed toward the people as a whole. These laws establish limitations on monarchy. There is no sovereignty even partially independent of the Torah's law. The king's duties and the king's behavior still had to pass the scrutiny of the Divine, although as indicated before, the Hasmonean kings were exempt from participation in the legal system, but the hallowed Davidic line was in theory or reality, who knows which, under the regulation of the Torah law.

The eventual rise of monarchs does not mean that a criminal justice system or a concept of crime comprehensible to us today or analogous to the modern concept of crime similarly arose. We do know that Solomon desired wisdom above all else, so that, *inter alia*, he could judge the people. And we know the famous

story of the custody case he adjudicated.[8] Moreover, we know
that the king had the power to suppress treason, with violence if
necessary, and to try and punish offenders against his dignity or
person. The estates of *haruge hamelekh* were forfeit to the Crown.[9]
Further, a system of lower and higher courts among the people,
in theory, dated from the time of Moses[10], and Davidic kings are
specifically included in this system.[11] This does not mean, however, that the monarch was also a genuine chief justice. That may
or may not have been the case. He did possess a rather broad
capital jurisdiction in homicide cases in which the Court of
Twenty-three was procedurally barred from prosecuting the suspected killer because no warning had been given or there was
only one witness, and so forth.[12] Royal duties as understood by
tradition principally fell into the fields of diplomacy, taxation,
foreign relations, and national defense. The question of the royal
person as chief magistrate is not explored in any detail in the
Maimonidean *Hilkhot Melakhim*.

The royal role in the justice system does not appear confined
only to matters touching the peace of the kingdom. Certainly
Solomon's wisdom in the custody case became legendary, but
such a situation hardly qualifies as a criminal matter in any catalog of crimes. Apparently the justice system, which treated all
causes without our familiar civil and criminal classifications, was
a separate entity in which the monarch participated. As Maimonides projected, there was a general system of courts founded
on the *beth din*, in which the king was not necessarily a chief
magistrate. At any rate such was Maimonides's view, based on
talmudic amplification of biblical material. Even the king, of
course, was not independent of censure under the system—
recall the experience of David we already noted.

It is, of course, understood that the views of Maimonides
come from a much later time and a far different place with
respect to the ancient monarchy and the rabbinic discussions of
that entity, already a far distant memory even in rabbinic times.
Nevertheless, the *Hilkoth Melakhim*, chapters two through six, are
particulary instructive. Would that we had some state archives of
the Davidic period, independent from what we have in Scripture. But we don't. We are forced into anachronism in order to
find some detail which amplifies the biblical descriptions of the
king's powers and privileges. The rabbinic discussion of such
biblical material contemplated a season long past, yet piously

expected to resume should it be the divine wish. Therefore what was proposed as the royal purview and power did not have purely theoretical value. Doubtless the rabbis could imagine a Davidic sovereign once more on the throne of the Jewish kingdom. The rules for the king had to be as specific and concrete as they could make them. Maimonides, almost a thousand years later, could also have contemplated the reemergence of an actual kingdom. And thus he clearly tries with all his enormous knowledge and skill to present the law pertaining to the monarchy as a practical as well as theoretical code. That the role of king as chief magistrate nowhere becomes clear therefore has some significance for this present inquiry.

The principal question for us to resolve is whether or not a concept of crime developed on the basis of any royal law. This also does not seem to have happened. No class of offenses appears to have become the special purview of the crown outside the obvious ones of *lèse majesté*, treason, and on occasion, murder. We are a long way from a notion of criminal justice as we understand it. Most of what we call crimes today remained essentially private quarrels, resolved by volunteer courts after the fashion of the ancient Mosaic model.

Further, concurrently with monarchy, and indeed predating it by a considerable length, we find the power of the priesthood, which maintained its own species of jurisdiction in matters of ritual and other areas. This type of authority was at least as significant, if not more so, in the context of the Religion State as the power of monarchy, not to mention local clan and tribal leaders. The priests after all ministered to God on behalf of the people, and the degree of lawlessness among the populace was certainly a major concern to them. The priesthood necessarily had to superintend the lawful and orderly practice of religion which the Torah placed at the center of human concerns. The realm of religion and the cult represents a part of a justice system at least complementary to royal law. After all, who was the ultimate Sovereign of the Jews if not God, whom the priests served with diligence?

We return to the question posed above, whether or not the ancient Jewish State played a role in the prosecution of wrongdoers. Let us leave aside the rabbinic projection of the *beth din* and the *sanhedrin* and so forth onto the ancient machinery of the Jewish monarchical state. That is a beloved traditional anachronism. But any answer to this question throws us into a time warp, and it becomes difficult to retain a firm grip on several important strands that really need to be followed in the pursuit of an answer.

First, the matter of the Religion State. If the Torah is the ancient constitution of our Religion State, and that Torah is the divine law, then the true sovereign of the Jewish people is God, not just in a theological sense, but in a jurisprudential sense. Our legal tradition clearly asserts the power of God to require punishment for transgression in a number of ways— including the payment of money, or valuable property and even the capital penalty. If, then, God is the sovereign, and God sets the punishments for wrongdoing, any offense against the Torah's law is tantamount to a crime in the modern sense. Indeed, the modern definition of crime includes the notion of offenses against Deity, no matter that the rabbis later remarked that God upon hearing a certain rabbinic opinion on the primary role of the rabbinic jurists in legal interpretation happily acknowledged *nitzhuni banai!*[13] What the rabbis did was to serve as the vicars of divine justice. They saw their role in the legal system not as independent agents of an independent legal system, but as the genuine and true masters of divine law to be administered as they in their most prayerful judgment saw fit to execute it. It would appear, therefore, that every offense in Jewish law becomes a crime simply because it is an offense against God, since God is the Sovereign whose power is coeval with the security and existence of the State. This criminalization, so to speak, of every wrongful act in Jewish law would hold good whether or not the system itself ever actually functioned at all at any time or at any place.

Second, in true *wissenschaftliche* style we should ask what the fields of comparative law and legal history might add to this inquiry into criminal law. Here is another strand of the time warp we encounter.

From Roman law and legal history we know that centuries elapsed from the early period until the development of a regular and professional judicial system.[14] Originally a judge was an upstanding citizen who was called upon to hear contending parties. The judge was an unpaid volunteer in this service. The Roman State very early assumed jurisdiction in matters of treason and murder and perhaps in some cases of false evidence. In approximately 100 BCE, the old system was revised and a group of paid magistrates were charged to hear cases involving violent acts, arson, etc. Moreover, permanent courts took over jurisdiction of cases of particularly grievous nature and cases which appeared to pose a danger to State security. Sulla recognized these permanent criminal courts and instituted six of them with jurisdiction over murder, poisoning, forgery of wills, high treason, bribery in elections, extortion by provincial governors, and embezzlement of public funds. By the end of the second century CE, the city prefect, an officer delegated by the emperor, handled all criminal complaints within 100 miles of Rome, and the praetorian prefect was the criminal magistrate elsewhere in Italy, and so forth.

The role of the State is very clear here. In the course of two centuries, more or less, the presence of the emperor as embodiment of the State had reached out to create a criminal justice system much like one that we would understand today.

In English law the criminal justice system began as a means of prosecuting offenses against the person and property of the sovereign, and of course the act of treason, and slowly over the centuries expanded to include many matters perceived as injurious to the peace of the realm.[15] What had once been private quarrels eventually came to the notice of the magistrates of the crown.

When we turn to Jewish law, and the Torah at its heart, we find another picture. The development of a criminal justice system in scripture appears to be frozen at a particular point in historical development. Here we encounter a time warp in which willful murder and other offenses appear to be punishable by death, but matters have not yet come to the point at which criminal law and civil law have become distinct fields. Cases which are clearly criminal matters to us, rape and robbery, are apparently handled by the same courts under much the same rules as so called "civil" matters. Indeed the Court of Twenty-Three handled homicide, but death penalty cases meant much more than homicide as we shall presently describe.

Moreover, we may see a partial parallel between the emergence of the judiciary in scripture what we observed from Roman history. Moses, upon the advice of Jethro, organized a system of lower and higher courts to hear the cases of the people. Moses could not carry the entire load of justice himself. The most difficult matters eventually came before Moses. Undoubtedly this program relied on unpaid judges who acted in response to the call of civic duty and perhaps Divine command mediated by

Moses. Moses hardly instituted a gigantic paid judicial bureau-cracy in the desert. At any rate, these magistrates heard all man-ner of quarrel. One system tended to everything, suggesting that no particular offense or set of offenses was any more injurious to public peace than any other offenses, with the possible exception of murder. All unlawful acts were offenses against God, presum-ably, but the notion of crime as a public offense against some political state is not present. We shall presently return to this point. But now we turn to another aspect of the subject.

The Torah prescribes a death penalty in certain situations.[16] These are the so-called *dine nefashot*, often taken as a sort of rough halakhic parallel to criminal law. Willful murder is, as men-tioned, one of them. When we look at the others, we find that they fall into three general categories. First there is an extensive list of sexual transgressions—various degrees of incest, adultery and perversion. Second, there is a series of offenses involving idolatry, false prophecy, Sabbath violation, and various other rit-ual offenses. Third, there is a group of death penalty offenses involving affronts to parents and supreme authority. One capital offense, kidnapping for sale as a slave, which reminds us of the Joseph story, does not appear to fall into the three categories but it may indicate a powerful aversion to the exposure of the victim to idolatrous acts and societies.

Let us note well that communal apostasy is on the list; this act amounts to treason against God.

In the traditional literature *kareth*—to the rabbis, death through some divine agency—is prescribed for similar lists of rit-ual and sexual offenses when the unlawful act has been willful but there was no formal procedural warning given to the offender.[17]

Thus, murder and a form of treason appear to have very deep roots in any Jewish concept of crime. They clearly upset the peace of the community and offend outrageously against God and the king for that matter. We should also note that *mesirah* became a capital crime as well in the course of time.[18] Particularly in medieval Jewish communities, the person who persistently and wantonly exposed Jewish lives and Jewish property to gentile depredations endangered the peace of the community which functioned as an *imperium in imperio*. The informer or traducer was identified with the "murderous pursuer" of the ancient law and thus liable to the severest punishment.

Let us, however, look again at these *dine nefashot*.

If they are criminal law, then what do we have in them? First, a catalog of sexual offenses and perversions that presumably upset the patriarchal and tribal structure of family and civic life in the Religion State. The significance of the extended family was paramount in the tribal community and so one imagines that whatever disturbed the proper lines of organization and property in a fundamental fashion required the most severe penalty. Second, the affronts to parents clearly cut the fabric of society most brutally, and could not be countenanced at all. And the third category of ritual offenses are manifestly offenses against the sovereign God. These are substantially the classes within the *dine nefashot*.

The catalog prompts two immediate questions. First where are such matters as battery, mayhem, rape, robbery, arson and the like? Second, is this list of death penalty offenses an adequate basis for asserting they are the analog to a concept of criminal law in the halakhah?

As for the first question, battery, mayhem, rape, arson and robbery are clearly criminal matters in the technical sense for us today. They are offenses against society and the welfare of the State. The State has jurisdiction in them. For Jewish law they are treated as *dine mamonot*, pecuniary judgements. These such cases are resolved by payment of money, fines, damages, mulcts, and the like. As a result of this *din mamon* status they are often lumped together with other pecuniary matters as "civil law" cases in scholarly and technical discussions of halakhah. Civil law of course comprehends what we today understand as matters of strict liability and contract. Yet obviously there is a difference between breaking someone's legs or blinding his eye and a quarrel between neighbors over the height of a fence or over dumping trash or over non-payment of rent for an apartment. They are manifestly different both in kind and degree altogether.

The categories of *dine nefashot* and *dine mamonot* simply will not do or analogs for criminal and civil law. We are better served if we understand them as categories peculiar to the halakhah, having no logical or jurisprudential link to the notions of "civil" and "criminal." Jewish law has its own technical terminology and its own categories. We should not try to translate the Jewish technical language into the technical language of other legal systems. There is no reason why the two languages should fit; and indeed they do not fit. The attempt misleads more than it clarifies.

Undoubtedly we find authors using the terms "civil" and "criminal" when writing of *dine mamonot* and *dine nefashot* because their training in Jewish law has been augmented by training in English law. The tendency for them to detect parallels and to use the terminology of one system in terms of the other is nigh irresistible. One clear example of this tendency appears in Emanuel Quint's *A Restatement of Rabbinic Civil Law*,[19] where it is clearly indicated at pp. 15-21, that the *beth din* has civil and not criminal jurisdiction. Examples could be easily multiplied.

Now the second question. Are the halakhic death penalty offenses a reasonable analog to the concept of criminal law? Clearly they are not. The *dine nefashot,* if indeed they were ever actually put into effect as they stand in scripture, reflect a period long before the State assumed a clear and significant role in criminal jurisdiction. Aside from murder and a possible form of treason, we have in this list essentially family matters, incest and so forth, that may or may not strike us today as criminal acts worthy of death. They may be prosecutable and they certainly are serious offenses, but do we look on them as capital matters?

Moreover, would we view the offense against parents and indeed the ritual offenses with the same horror as did our ancestors? I think not. We might see them as serious and grievous but hardly as deadly. We live in a different world, and what the Torah declares to be deadly affronts to society and God are for us both too few (where are mayhem and rape?) and too remote (idolatry is no longer part of our real world).

We possess an ancient and beloved tradition that speaks in its own language. In the area of crime and criminal jurisdiction its progress in many areas halted ages ago. It preserves a catalog of offenses against a religion and tribal society. These are the deadly sins. In the course of time, the rabbis preserved the old list and expanded upon the ancient legal heritage, but they could not really add to the scriptural list of serious crimes. Even the kings of Israel do not appear to have done so, no matter what they might have done for their self-protection and the protection of their repose on the throne.[20] The State does not appear to have grown to a stature where it could assume the awesome task of criminal jurisdiction. The most grievous acts between persons, that we would not hesitate for a moment to call "criminal," remained individual quarrels to be adjusted among individuals by payment of money or other nonlethal procedures.

An ever-present question, particularly among liberal Jews, is whether this notion of capital punishment—*dine nefashot*—is it part of our system. Of course it is. We are properly proud of R. Eliezer b. Azariah, R. Tarfon and R. Akiba who clearly and eloquently opposed the death penalty, but we stop short of Rabban Shimon b. Gamaliel's retort, "They would have even multiplied shedders of blood in Israel."[21] Years ago, Prof. Julius Kravetz expressed a similar point in a CCAR *Journal* article, citing unimpeachable sources to correct the view that halakhah fully comports with the most liberal of twentieth century notions in criminal law.[22] The point is clearly there for all to ponder. Shimon b. Shetah certainly thought capital punishment was part of the system.[23] Various rabbis in the medieval communities of Spain spoke out eloquently for capital and corporal punishment, and their rules of procedure did not even require the safeguards of the classic *dine nefashot* prosecution in their own day.[24] Capital jurisdiction in its classic form disappeared as a live option in the Jewish state in Roman times well before the year 70; that much is history.[25] And the rabbis had the luxury of voicing moral criticism of the death penalty without the burden of any duty to enforce their criminal justice system such as it was. We may condemn capital punishment today for a variety of very sound reasons. Our invocation of the Jewish legal tradition in that cause is severely flawed at best.

As for the concept of crime, when we bring all the strands together we have something like this. First, our Jewish legal heritage embodied in the halakhah represents an ancient system that reflects an incredibly complex development even to our own day. It encountered virtually every social, political, economic and religious phenomenon of the western world, and it found a way to respond and function in the presence of each of them. The system has its own terminology and its own classification of legal matters. We translate the halakhah's program and vocabulary into the vernacular of another system at our peril. Of course, some aspects of halakhah have in the last century become identified as a, so to speak, secular body of Jewish law, that can be compared to other secular systems or that can be forged into modern law for a western style secular state. This body of material is called *Mishpat Ivri*[26], but *Mishpat Ivri* is certainly not halakhah and there is no doubt on that point.

Crime is understood today as a public offense, an offense against the peace and welfare of the State. Therefore the State assumes the principal role in suppressing and prosecuting crime. As we noted early on, however, the definition of crime also includes offenses against divine law, and in Jewish tradition much of the Torah is unabashedly presented as divine law.

Ancient Israelite polity, whether tribal or monarchical, was fundamentally a Religion State. The cult was the unifying factor among the people. In perhaps more exalted terms, the proper task of Jews, no matter of what rank or station, was to serve God wholeheartedly through the cult. Religion was the focus and foundation of the people. The Torah with all its complexity was clearly perceived as the divine revelation that informed the Jews how they were to serve God in every aspect of their lives. Thus, any offense against the laws of the Torah may be properly seen as an offense against God, and therefore, in our language—a crime. This concept is not of course made explicit in so many words—crime is not a halakhic term—in the Torah, but breaking a law of the Torah at a bare minimum must be an affront to Deity. Thus we have a sort of implicit concept of crime on the basis of Torah: a crime is an offense against the Divine, and that idea covers broad territory.

The problem with this concept is simply that it is too broad. It becomes virtually meaningless in the modern world. If every offense is a crime, then criminal law is the only law, and that will not translate into viable modern language, particularly in the areas of ritual law and personal status which range far afield from any criminal connotation in the legal systems of modern states.

The Torah, so we understand, was amplified and adjusted, but not technically changed in form or substance, by centuries of rabbinic legal debate and decision. Since the rabbis could not and surely would not dismiss ancient divine law in favor of legislation of their own making, despite what we may wish to detect in their finely spun arguments, we find the halakhah working with any number of ancient institutions and notions that had long fallen into disuse. No matter; Torah was Torah and the entire corpus, ancient concepts and institutions along with later rabbinic ideas and forms reframed through rabbinic debate, were passed along to succeeding generations.

The rabbis, for their part did not govern an independent polity. Whether they functioned under Hasmonean kings, or Roman imperial governors, they were not the masters of the State. The idea of crimes as offenses against the political state, was not at all their primary concern, and so the ancient death penalties of the Religion State were interpreted out of existence. When the rabbis did, however, find themselves facing a sufficiently serious offense against religion, they did not hesitate to inflict the capital sentence. Ask Simon b. Shetah about that, or Eliezer b. Jacob.[27]

But the Jewish people, without a State of their own, did not and could not develop their law to the point at which some offenses became crimes in the modern sense of the term. The old death penalty Court of Twenty-Three no longer functioned, and its memory prompted Akiba and Tarfon and others to decry capital punishment. Yet all manner of acts which we would clearly understand as criminal remained under the purview of the rabbinical courts, which were not an arm of political sovereignty. The system, without the element of political power, did not and could not begin to classify offenses as civil and criminal in their modern senses, or in their medieval or Roman senses for that matter. The system was, as it were, frozen in time, on one side bound by ineluctable sacred ties to the past, and on the other by the absence of political power to develop anything resembling our present and secular notion of criminal law. Until 1948, no secular authority emerged among the Jews, either in concert with the *beth din* or in addition to it, to assume jurisdiction over various offenses which threatened the peace of the State or the well-being of its citizens.

So then, is there a concept of crime or not? From the point of view of religion, there was and is the offense against Deity. Of course, the precise nature of such offenses is also detailed in Torah, and that detailing eliminates much that we would now call crime and includes much that we would not.

In this discussion of the concept of crime, the matter of punishment necessarily received some attention. A few further observations on punishment are in order now that the matter of crime has been explored as to its meaning and basis.

About twenty years ago, a book entitled, *The Search for Criminal Man* appeared: it is subtitled, *A Conceptual History of the Dangerous Offender*.[28] This book, by Ysabel F. Rennie, is an absorbing study of the literature on crime and criminology from the ancient and medieval periods down through the enlightenment and into the modern period. It demonstrates how perceptions of crime and criminals were influenced by the thought of Bentham, Rousseau,

Marx, Freud and other seminal thinkers of western civilization. It is also an easy read, which was most pleasant.

First, the author notes that "the criminal justice system of all countries flows from the classical tradition, which assumes that people are free agents and that when they transgress the law they deserve to be punished. There is nothing that makes the average law enforcement officer more impatient than claims that the criminal is the victim of society. If police, prosecutors, and judges accept any determinism at all, it is the biological determinism that claims some people are by nature too dangerous to be at large.

Further, we find the remark that "where law posits free will, criminology, both biogenic and sociogenic posits determinism. Where the law sees a criminal who acts rationally, criminology sees someone who does not—who is in fact driven by forces beyond his control or understanding."[29]

What then of Jewish Law? What then of the notion of offenses against Deity that appears to be our classic analog to the idea of crime and its punishment? Surely we believe in free will and individual responsibility. The offender who is mentally unfit to stand trial can be dealt with in various ways, but our tradition for the most part views an unlawful act—civil, criminal, ritual or what have you—as the result of a free choice on the part of the offender. Certainly there is the *yetzer hara* that prompts people to do wrong, but there are also the *yetzer hatov* and the guidance of religion to steer the potential offender away from sin. When the act is, despite all conflicting influences, performed, the war of the *yetzarim* is over, the person is viewed as a rational actor.

Ms Rennie concludes with the remark that the reason we argue fruitlessly over what should be done with criminals is that we can not agree on who and what is man.[30] This is a vital observation that one is inclined to dismiss as too glib. We should, however, be careful not to dismiss it. Much that we do and say takes its justification from our views, personal or communal, of what a human being is or is supposed to be. The law comes with its precedents and common sense and we have one view of humanity; criminology comes with data and we have another view. The fundamental problem in crime and punishment is at bottom philosophical.

The masters of halakhah did not have the benefit, if it is a benefit, of criminological data. They clearly incline to the view that crime is somehow an act of volition, misguided and wrong, but volition none the less. Our confessions on Yom Kippur become nonsense without free will.

The same author concludes her book with these comments. "In the mental storehouse where penologists keep their theories, there should be a sign clearly posted above each storage bin: Warning! this idea was tried in the _____, _____, and _____, centuries and did not work."[31] She portrays the fact that no matter what we say about crime, criminals, punishment and the causes of crime, it has all been said before and nothing has ever worked very well to suppress or eliminate crime. Crime and criminals are still with us.

Perhaps, as the author suggests in so many words, we would be best served simply to assert that the purpose of criminal justice is simply criminal justice.[32] When we speak of criminal justice we are unendingly engulfed in philosophical quicksand if we search for prevention of crime or its cure, or the abolition of crime or some other utopian end.

I submit to you that the rabbis perceived the purpose of justice in terms quite different from modern discussions of the subject. They often wanted justice to be exemplary and they always wanted to seek some tangible redress for the victim, but they also strove to extinguish the fires of sin and bring all litigants to a truly God-fearing state; hardly the stuff of modern criminology or penology. When they dispensed justice they had their rules and their laws of Torah. They might apply then with more or less rigor. They were as a rule persons of compassion and wisdom and they did not usually wield the law as bludgeon. There are some exceptions, however, when a rabbi's personal dignity or sense of self suffered affront.[33] They by and large dispensed justice on the footing that the accused before them acted freely and he or she would have to prove otherwise to escape a just verdict and sentence, and the necessity of sincere repentance.

The Jewish concept of crime, if one may fairly say it exists, is inadequate in a modern state. Our law did not have the space and freedom necessary to develop a concept of crime as such. Fundamentally we only know of grave offenses which may be against persons, but are certainly against God. This antique notion may not serve a functioning legal system in a modern society, but it never hampered the cause of justice itself, civil or criminal. The rabbis strove to achieve what was right and good when they sat in judgment. With great consistency they achieved that goal in their own times through use of modes and methods quite far removed from our secular and western approach to crime and punishment. Their success was notable, gained as it often was under adverse social circumstances, involving contentious community factions and the ever-watchful, and often hostile, eye of gentile authority upon them. Their system, moreover, did not require them to employ ideas like civil and criminal and criminal justice and crime in their endeavors. We should not ask of our ancestors any more than the noble efforts they made and their signal achievements in the pursuit of justice. We certainly can not ask them to present a concept of crime that satisfies the modern legal mind or that fits a definition framed far away from the thunderous revelation at Sinai.

Notes

I am grateful to my colleague Professor David Ellenson who read the manuscript of this paper and offered several valuable suggestions.

1. I have dealt with such topics as reasonable cause arrest, "Reflections on Reasonable Cause in Halakha," *Jewish Law Association Studies* VI (1990); "The Berure Averot and the Administration of Justice in XIII and XIV Century Spain," *Jewish Law Association Studies*, IV (1990); "The Use of Excessive Force by a Peace Officer," *Jewish Law Association Studies* I (1985); and an extensive monograph, "Aspects of Physical Violence Against Persons in Karo's Shulhan Arukh," *Jewish Law Annual* IX (1991).
2. See, for instance, California Penal Code, chapters 15, 16, and 17.
3. Reference here is to the classic "we shall do and we shall hearken" and the midrash thereon, Exodus 24:7, see e.g. *Toledot Aaron*, and *Pesikta Rabbati*.
4. Shabbat 88a.
5. 2 Samuel 12.
6. *Hilkhoth Melakhim* 3:7, amplifying M. Sanhedrin 2:2.
7. Deuteronomy 16:18; note however that in the next verse, the instructions on the administration of justice are addressed to individual judges.
8. 1 Kings 3:16-28.
9. *Hilkhoth Melakhim* 4:9 cp. 3:8.
10. The famous advice of Jethro, Exodus 18:13-26.
11. Cp. *supra* n.6.

12. *Hilkhoth Melakhim* 3:10.
13. See Baba Metzia 59 b.
14. For easy reference, see O. Telegen-Couperus, *A Short History of Roman Law*, Routledge (London: 1993), pp. 50ff.
15. See, e.g. E. Pollock and F.W. Maitland, *History of English Law Before the Time of Edward First*, 2 vols., Cambridge University Press (Cambridge: 1968).
16. See M. Sanhedrin 7:4, 9:1, *inter alia*.
17. M. Keritot 1:1. See the commentary of Bertinoro *ad loc.*
18. See for instance, J. Bazak and S. Passamaneck, *Jewish Law and Jewish Life*, Book 7, Union of American Hebrew Congregations (New York: 1977), pp. 25-37.
19. Vol. 1, Northvale: 1990.
20. *Hilkhoth Melakim* 3:8.
21. M. Makkot 1:10; see Richard Block, *infra.* pp. 84-85.
22. Julius Kravetz, "Some Cautionary Remarks," *Central Conference of American Rabbis Journal*, XV no. 1: 1968 pp. 75-81.
23. Sanhedrin 45 b.
24. See Stephen M. Passamaneck, "R. Judah b. Asher on Capital Penalties," *Jewish Law Association Studies*, VII: 1994.
25. N.S. Hecht, *et. al.*, *Introduction to the History and Sources of Jewish Law*, Clarendon Press (Oxford: 1996), p. 103.
26. N.S. Hecht *et. al.*, *op. cit.*, pp. 398f. and pp. 416f.
27. See Sanhedrin 45 b and, regarding R. Eliezer b. Yaakov, B. Sanhedrin 46 a.
28. Ysabel F. Rennie, *The Search for Criminal Man: A Conceptual History of the Dangerous Offender*, D.C. Heath and Co. (Lexington, MA: 1978).
29. Ysabel F. Rennie, *The Search for Criminal Man*, p. 147.
30. Ibid., 149f.
31. Ibid., 274.
32. Ibid.
33. See S.M. Passamaneck, "The Talmudic Concept of Defamation" in *Studies in Jewish Jurisprudence*, vol. 4, ed. byAbraham M. Fuss (New York: 1976), pp. 41-48.

Chapter 2

❖   ❖   ❖

WHAT IS CRIME?

Leonard Kravitz

What is a crime? That originally was not a Jewish question. Jews did not speak of crimes; they spoke *of chait, averah. pesha*, of sins of various kinds, the kinds of sins for which we will beat our breasts this coming Yom Kippur as we repeat the long confessional: *ashamnu, bagadnu, gazalnu, debarnu dofi.* "Crime" is a secular term; sin is a religious term. We Jews dealt with sins; crimes were the things that other people dealt with. I should like to speak about the transformation of sin into crime and the transformation of crimes into sins. Perhaps a paradox, but "a most unusual paradox."

I will begin with a definition. Crime is

1. the commission of an act that is forbidden or the omission of a duty that is commanded by a public law and that makes the offender liable to punishment by that law ...
2. a grave offense especially against morality
3. criminal activity ...
4. something reprehensible, foolish , or disgraceful.[1]

Notes for this section begin on page 32.

Crime, according to the first definition is that which is defined by a public body and which is punished by that body. The linkage between definition and punishment, we shall see, is crucial; without it, crime becomes merely the second definition given, viz., something against morality or, even worse, that which the fourth definition speaks of, something foolish or disgraceful.

The "public body" spoken of suggests some kind of societal structure which can both enact and punish. It should be clear that any such structure is both time and place bound. Crime is what a particular society at a particular time says is crime. Thus, what may be a crime at one time may not be a crime at another; or, what may be a crime in one place at one particular time, may not be a crime in other place at the same time. The same is true with the other definitions: what may be morality at one time may not be morality at another time and what may not be moral in one place at one time may be moral in another place at the same time. Crime, whether defined as that which will be punished or that which will be viewed with opprobrium, is the result of human reflection on human actions and as such, changes as human beings change.

Sin is a different matter, so it seems. An old edition of the Jewish Encyclopedia made the distinction between sin and crime in the following manner:

> Crime [is] ... An act forbidden by human Law and punished human authority, in contrast to sinful acts which are thought to be evil in the eyes of God.[2]

"Evil in the eyes of God"!? That does not sound like something as changeable! *An averah bleibt an avera*, my zaida, my grandfather, might have said. An *averah*, a *pesha*, a *chait* is something which the Torah prohibits since the Torah comes from God and *lo yahalif Ha–El velo yamir dato*, God does not change and His Torah does not change, and a sin remains a sin!

Or does it? I would like to argue that what has happened in Jewish life is that sins have become crimes and crimes have become sins. The paradox with which I began will be explainable when we understand that what is true about crime is also true about sin; what we think is sin changes depending on time and place. The certainty that sin is that which is evil in the eyes of God has been lost; sin, like crime, may be an "... offense ... against morality" or, "something reprehensible" but that morality or that sense of reprehensibility depends upon a particular group's understanding of what is right and wrong and that sense of right and wrong, alas, is something that changes. Lest we think that such a notion is terribly modern, a product of these immoral times, let me quote a medieval thinker by the name of Efodi, who lived around 1391 and was a commentator on Maimonides' *Guide for the Perplexed*. Maimonides in Part One, Chapter Two, discusses the differences between statements which deal with things true and false and things which are good and evil. Maimonides places the latter into the category of *mefursamot*, "conventional" or "apparent" truths. Efodi, comments that if there were no people, there would be no *mefursamot* and goes on to way that good and evil are by *haskamat anashim*, human convention.[3]

To say that human convention determines what is good and evil is to say a great deal about what a particular Jewish philosopher thought about traditional belief [though this is not the time or place to expound my view of Maimonides or his commentators!] It is to say that if good and evil are determined by human convention, then it follows that what is considered "crime" is also determined by human convention.[4]

Let me return to the linkage between crime and punishment. Without punishment, there can be no crimes That is what makes transactions between nations problematical. If crime is that which is forbidden by a "public law" and punishable by that law, we find that nation-states do not fit within the "public" of one another and therefore cannot be "punished" by one another. What one nation does to another may be considered a crime, in the sense of a matter of opprobrium by the one who suffers, but obviously will not be so considered by the one who acts. Moreover, only if the nation that suffers can somehow punish the one which acted against it will what was done be considered a crime in the full sense of the word. The International Court of Justice in the Hague, for example, has no ability to punish the most powerful country in the world; hence, the United States can maintain a blockade against Cuba, which might otherwise be considered a crime against international law. Such a blockade is not considered by us or by most of the world as a crime, any more than the forming, arming, and financing of the "Contras" against Nicaragua was viewed as crime. Our actions against Cuba and Nicaragua are viewed merely as acts of foreign policy.

To apply the notion of "crime" to nations one needs a supra-national body to declare that certain actions are crimes. The Nuremberg Trials, held after the Second World War, were attempts, even though they might have been viewed as an *ex post facto* pro-cedures, to declare that certain actions of the Nazi government, however licit they may have seemed to that government, were, in fact, crimes. Beyond the seemingly obvious crime of genocide, alas so often part of human history, the Nuremberg Tribunal held that offensive wars were also crimes. One might wonder what would have happened if the *ex post facto* process had been con-tinued and those sitting in judgement had been judged for hav-ing committed the crime of offensive warfare!

Offensive wars, particularly wars of conquest, have played their role in the history of nations and in Jewish history as well, though the Jews were to develop the notion that there was some-thing above all nations, a Being that was above and beyond all things, God, the King of Kings and the Lord of Lords—that notion was used to justify the conquest of Canaan. (Whether in fact, the Children of Israel actually conquered Canaan in the manner described in Scripture is another matter!) Rashi, the great commentator on the Bible, explains how that conquest was not a crime, not even in the sense of being "an offense ... against morality" by quoting the Midrash: God Who created the world and all that is in it can give any part of the world to whomsoever He chooses! Thus we Jews were saved from the charge: *listim atem*! "Ye are bandits."[4]

The notion of the God of the entire world directing one nation to conquer another is known to us as Americans. It was "manifest destiny," obviously directed from on High, that per-mitted us to take over the land of the Indians. I am reminded of an exhibit I saw at the Army Museum at the Presidio in San Fran-cisco. It dealt with the Indian wars and had the most interesting title: "A Clash of Cultures"—as if the issue between the compet-ing groups was a disagreement about art or music!

God had created the world, according to the Torah, in order to place human beings within it and to arrive at a specific group of human beings, those descended from Abraham, which group would ultimately become the Jewish People. That belief would be embellished by the Midrash to suggest that the idea of the Jewish People was linked to the Torah in the proceeding cre-ation.[5] Thus Torah, the Jewish People, and creation were linked.

Not only creation was linked to that people; the world's ongoing existence was also so linked, for had Israel not accepted the Torah, the world would have returned to nothingness and void.[6] Thus in the Jewish mind of the past, the Torah was as enduring as the world and it could no more change than God could change, God could not change, the Torah could not change, the Jewish people could not change: "For I the Lord change not; And ye, O sons of Jacob, are not consumed."[7]

But the Jewish people did change and the way that the Torah was read also changed. That change was due in part to the Enlightenment, though it was anticipated by some medieval thinkers. That change was simply to read the Torah in particular and the Bible in general as one read any other book, without any presuppositions. In so doing, it was discovered that the Bible was written down long after the events depicted, in some cases evincing viewpoints in the writing different from what might have been expected from events the depicted. The Torah reflected different traditions which were put together in different strands.

Rabbinic literature, which commented upon and expanded the biblical literature, viewed from the modern angle of vision was seen to manifest development and change; it can no longer be thought of as spinning effortlessly and inexorably from the biblical texts upon which it was built.

Both biblical and rabbinic literature reflected different times and different places. It followed that the legal aspect of those literatures paralleled the development of other legal literatures. In his magisterial study of Jewish law, Menachem Elon observed that, "'religious' law and 'legal' law in the *Halakhah* are of one piece, and this is not merely because they have a common source. The analytical approach, the terminology, the methods of interpretation, and all other methods of halakhic clarification and creativity characterize the entire body of the *Halakhah*."[8]

One could draw the conclusion that the reason that the so-called religious law and the so-called legal law followed similar patterns was because they both reflect how human beings operate. With that in mind, we can look back at traditional texts and see things that before we might have missed. For example, though we know from the Midrash that the acceptance of the Torah by the Jewish People was forced, that otherwise Mt Sinai would have been dropped on their heads,[9] there is another view that made that acceptance voluntary, based on the notion of a rational *quid pro quo*:

"To what may this be compared To ... a king who entered a province and said to the people: May I be your king? But the people said to him: Have you done anything good for us ...? What did he do then? He built the city wall ... he brought in the water supply ... [and] he fought their battles .... He said .... May I be your King? They said, yes .... Likewise God. He brought the Israelites out of Egypt, divided the Sea for them, sent down manna .... He fought for them .... Then He said ... I am to be your King. And they said to Him, Yes, Yes."[10]

Even for the Rabbis, then, the acceptance of the Torah was an act akin to other human acts and gained its intelligibility from parallels with those acts. Even so, what the Rabbis might not have seen, or having seen, might not have wished to say, we can say: Law, indeed, the law of the Torah, is a function of human creativity. Human creativity, however, differs from place to place and from time to time. That conclusion has its impact on what was and is considered sin and what was and is considered crime. It would seem that on logical grounds alone, sin cannot be considered something unchanging; sin reflects the same variability as crime.

Sin is purported to have a divine declaration as its source; crime was thought to be that proscribed by a human court. That human court had to be set in a particular group and control a particular area in order to maintain and enforce jurisdiction. The history of the Jewish People is such that jurisdictions changed as group and area changed. The biblical text tells of the formation of the people, from individuals to clans to tribes to a people, to a people divided, to a people ravaged, to a people exiled, to a people restored, to a people once again in exile. Thus the people are in the Land and outside it and in it and outside it again. The Jewish People is formed and commanded by the Torah; yet even in the Land, there are other peoples. The interactions between members of the Jewish People and others are at times covered and at time not covered by similar expections, so that negative interactions are at times considered "crimes" and at times not.

To return to God: that term and the term "fear of God," both of which may be anachronistic retrojection, serve as indicators of a common bond between the Hebrews and others. Thus Abraham excuses his telling Avimelech that Sarah was his sister and not his wife by saying that, "... there is no fear of God in the place."[11] Joseph fends off Mrs. Potiphar by saying, "How could I

... sin before God."[12] Joseph as Egyptian vizier, having recognized his brothers while they did not recognize him, toys with them saying, "... I am a God fearing man."[13] It would seem that "fear of God" presents sufficient commonality to make certain actions "crimes," if not in terms of law, then in terms of opprobrium.

No such opprobrium relates to the actions of Jacob's sons at Shechem. Simon and Levi to revenge the rape and abduction of their sister Dina, kill not only Shechem who raped her, but his father Hamor and all the people of their city. The same people, one should remember, were willing to be circumcised that the Children of Israel might live among them. Father Jacob condemns their act not because it is a "crime," but because that act may presents difficulties for him. The Torah has him say, "... You have troubled me to make me odious among those who dwell in the land, the Canaanite and the Perizzite, while I am few in number, and if they gather against me and smite me, I and my household will be destroyed."[14]

Jacob' reaction is pure self-interest, not revulsion at the commission of a crime. Oddly enough, the response of the brothers bespeaks an implicit universal claim. Said they, "Shall one make our sister like a whore."[15] Though no legislation is spoken of, there is an element of punishment implied which suggests that their action was punishment for a crime: if one treats a woman as a whore, one deserves what one gets.

Crime and punishment suggest control: the biblical text will suggest that there were times when we were under our own control and at times under the control of others. At times, our law applied and at times their law applied. In the Book of Esther, we read Haman's complaint, "There is a certain people scattered abroad ... and their laws are diverse from those of every people; neither keep they the king's law ...."[16]

One could argue that Haman came to that conclusion because Mordecai committed a crime by not following the king's command and not prostrating himself before Haman![17] Perhaps, but most of us would not consider Mordecai's actions to be a "crime" because we would not have accepted the kind of law which Haman assumed, even though the Jewish People as depicted in the Book of Esther were outside the land, living among others.

There were times, when living inside the Land, the Jews were unable to prevent others imposing their laws upon Jews. We read in the Mekhilta: Rabbi Eleazar, the son of Azariah, says,

"Now suppose the gentile courts judge according to the law of Israel. I might suppose that their decisions are valid [*kayamim*]. But Scripture says, 'And these are the Ordinances which thou shalt set before them.' You may judge their cases, but they are not to judge your cases."[18] Non-Jewish courts, even in a Jewish land, could compel Jews to do their bidding and could do so by force. The Mekilta passage goes on to say, "A bill of divorce given by force, if by an Israelitish authority is valid, but if by gentile authority is not valid. It is, however, valid if the Gentiles merely bind the husband over (*hobtin oto*, lit., 'beat him') saying to him, 'Do as the Israelites tell thee.'"[19]

The relation of Jews to the courts of non-Jews and with that the relation of Jews to that proscribed by those courts as crimes were to be problematic. Samuel, a first generation Babylonian Amora developed the doctrine of *dina d'malkhuta dina*: the law of the land is law. Elon, who gives a full discussion of the doctrine, presents a rather straightforward rationale for it given by the medieval legalist, Nissan of Gerundi, who said," Because the land is his and he [the king] could say to them [the Jews],"'If you don't obey my laws, I will expel you from my country.'"[20]

Thus obedience to the law of the country is presented as a pragmatic (in every sense) trade-off: to remain in the country, Jews will avoid doing anything prohibited by *their* law. One may wonder whether the doing of that which is prohibited would be internalized as committing a *crime*, i.e., something against morality or something reprehensible, or thought of as a merely breaking one of *their* laws? Would it be a matter of opprobrium or merely a matter of inconvenience?

For Rabbenu Nissim and for Jews throughout the world, *their* laws were theirs, touching Jews mainly as members of a separate community. *Their* law was *their* law and our law was our law. Jews were under Jewish law, with courts, judges, and the sanctions of this world as well of the next.

The French Revolution was to make the law of the country the law of the Jews. The Emancipation of the Jews meant that the Jew would become what he had not been since Roman times, a citizen. Being a citizen meant following French law like any other Frenchman. At the Napoleonic Sanhedrin of 1806-07, among the questions put to the Jewish notables were: "Do Jews born in France consider France their country? Are they willing to defend it and obey its laws?"[21]

For the first time, being in a country was for the Jew what it had been for others, the possibility of entry into citizenship. Citizenship carried a price, namely, the dissolution of separate status. One of Napoleon's representatives to the Sanhedrin, Portalis, *fils*, stated what now seems obvious: "The Jews have ceased to be a people and remained only a religion."[22] "Only a religion" could not retain and maintain a separate legal system. Law for all Frenchmen, Catholic or Protestants, Jews and nonbelievers, would be in theory the same.[23] What would be a crime for the one would be a crime for the other.

The French pattern of Emancipation was replicated throughout Western Europe. The new situation would create modern Judaism of every persuasion, in that whatever Judaism one adhered to was the Judaism that one chose. One could be and one can be any kind of Jew or no kind of Jew. Jewish law exists, but it cannot compel; it can only persuade, and it can only persuade those who are willing to be persuaded. Judaism can provide guidance for those who wish to accept that guidance.

To be a Jew in the modern world means to live in two cultural worlds and in one legal world. We can bring insights from Judaic sources to reflect upon and even evaluate the laws of our society, as we did with the "Jim Crow" laws, but until they are changed, we are bound by those laws. They can declare what is a crime and what is not, because the society through its courts can punish those who break those laws.

Sins have become in the modern world, that which is not or cannot be punished, because in an open society with different religious traditions, sin is that which is proscribed by a particular faith. Sin, therefore, is a private matter Whether eating ham or having an abortion, the sinfulness of the particular act depends on the religious position of the individual. Even if something is proscribed by a particular text, whether it is viewed as a sin will depend on the particular individual reading the text. The issue of homosexuality comes to mind. Prohibited by the Torah, homosexuality was a sin in past.[24] Present sensibility, based on new information that such a condition in not voluntary, does not call it a sin. Hence for modern Jews, homosexuality, whatever it may be, is not a sin.

Conversely, there are things in the Torah as interpreted by the tradition that would seem to us as moderns to be both a sin and a crime. Hence, though we might smile, when we read

Rashi's calculation of the nuptial age of Isaac and Rebecca as forty for him and three for her, [25] we know that any man of such an age who would attempt to marry a child of three and any person who would assist the accomplishment of such a marriage would be committing a particularly heinous crime.

Sin has changed; crime has changed. We bring a different sensibility to our reading of the sacred texts of the past, even the Torah. There are passages in it which to our modern minds command "Crimes, the kind of crimes which our age would call "crimes against humanity," though, alas, the world, even now, shows that they are still committed! I think of the problematic section in *Mattot* [26] which contains the commandment to exact revenge against the Midianites by slaying every male and every female old enough to engage in sexual intercourse. I am thankful that there are no Midianites at present. I used to think that were they suddenly to appear, no Jew would he willing to carry out such a commandment. Then Baruch Goldstein appeared on the scene, and he was followed by Yigal Amir and now I am not sure.

It is because I have a different sense of what is a sin and what is a crime and because I bring a different ethic and a different sense of history to the reading of the past, that I produce different answers to the question of sins and crimes. If on the simplest ethical level, "what I forbid another, I forbid myself and what I permit myself, I permit to another," I find that the commandment to commit genocide against the Midianite unacceptable. To accept the commandment to do the same to the Hittites, the Amorites, the Canaanites, the Peruzzites, the Hivites, and the Jebusites"[27] seems to me to make permissible the Holocaust, the attempted genocide of the Jewish People. To argue that for us, such a commandment was/is permissible because it is written in a book which we hold to be sacred is to forget the Holocaust against us was first intimated in a book, *Mein Kampf*, held sacred by Nazis! What was a crime against us surely would be a crime by us.

In sum: Efodi was right. Good and evil and therefore what is a crime is determined by *haskamat anashim*, anarchy, by human convention. Crime will depend on time and place; crime will depend on who does what to whom. The genius of the Jewish People was to link crime to sin, so that some things which people thought were wrong were held to be wrong in the eyes of God. To be honest they did not always work it out. They came up with

another idea, too: that there would be a time when there would
be no crime, a time when one could recline under one's fig tree
and none would make them afraid.[28] May it come soon!

Notes

1. Merriam Webster, New Collegiate Dictionary, 10th Ed. (Springfield, Mass: 1998), p. 274.
2. The Jewish Encyclopedia, Vol. 4 (New York: 1910), p. 357.
3. Efodi in Maimon *Hasefardi b'haatakat Shemuel Ibn-Tibbon*, Vol. 1 (Jerusalem 1960), p. 16b. A later commentator, Shem Tov, reading Efodi, wrote that truth dealt with things that are necessarily existent of which we are not the source, *shain anahnu sipatainu*, while "good and evil" dealt with that of which we are the source.
4. Rashi on Genesis 1:1.
5. Bereshit Rabba 1:5
6. B Shabbat 84a and elsewhere.
7. Malachi 3:6
8. Elon, Menachem, *Jewish Law: History, Sources, Principles*, Vol.1 (Philadelphia: 1982), p. 109.
9. B.Shabbat 88a; Jacob Z. Lauterbach (ed.) *Mekilta de Rab Ishmael* (Philadelphia: 1949), Vol. 2, Tractate Bakhodesh, Chapter 5, p. 219.
10. Ibid., pp. 229, 230.
11. Gen. 20:11.
12. Gen. 39:9.
13. Gen. 42:18.
14. Gen. 34:30.
15. Gen. 34:31.
16. Esther 3:8.
17. Esther 3:2.
18. Lauterbach, *Mekhilta.*, Vol 3, Tractate Nezikin, 1 pp. 1, 2. p. 2, Note 1, provides the following comment: "In the Israelitish Commonwealth only fully qualified citizens, priests, Levites, and Israelites, could hold the office of judge. They could judge cases of non-Israelitish residents, but a non-Israelite, i.e., a foreigner who has not accepted the Jewish religion and hence was not a fully qualified citizen could not function as a judge in a Jewish state." (See M. Sanh.4:2, Sanh.36b and Kid 76b and commentaries). What Lauterbach did not say was that the Jews being under Roman rule could not control who could or could not be a judge in the Jewish commonwealth and the Mekhilta passage expresses more of a hope than a reality.
19. Ibid.
20. Elan, *Jewish Law*, Vol.1, p. 65 and note #45.

21. Sachar, Howard M., *The Course of Modern Jewish History* (Cleveland, New York: 1958) p. 60.
22. Ibid., 63.
23. Elon, *Jewish Law*, Vol. 4, pp. 1576–88, describes the response of various rabbinic authorities to the loss of juridical autonomy. One phrase, quoted of a Jewish traveler of the time stands out: "In his [Napoleon's] days, the Jewish People, while delighted by their new physical freedom, were stunned by the their new spiritual slavery" (p. 1582, note #15). It goes without saying that not all Jews, as evinced by their moving out from under the umbrella of Jewish jurisprudence, agreed with that statement.
24. Lev.18:22 and 20:13.
25. In his comment on Gen. 25.2.
26. Numbers 31.
27. Deut. 20:17.
28. Micah 4:4.

Chapter 3

❖   ❖   ❖

ASSISTING THE GUILTY
Halakhic Considerations

Clifford E. Librach

As a modern American rabbi serving in a suburban metropoli-
tan congregation,[1] I have been routinely exposed to the delicate
problems of individuals, some of which involve criminal behavior. Specifically, my experience as a congregational rabbi and
advisor to colleagues has brought to me the following personal
crises of people whom we have served in the past.[2] One individual revealed and confessed criminal complicity in a scheme to
harbor an illegal alien and thereby to defraud federal and state
authorities, participating in a criminal scheme of misrepresenta-
tion; another individual sought spiritual guidance during the
course of which he revealed his own criminal culpability in a
complicated enterprise of bank fraud involving real estate sales
to middle income households; and, in perhaps the most difficult
case, I was faced with the evident confession by a father to the
routine physical abuse of his children.

In this paper, I propose to address the halakhic considerations involving an appropriate professional response to these

---

Notes for this section begin on page 42.

real crises.[3] Specifically, I will discuss problems involved in (a) defending one accused of a crime, (b) informing secular authorities of criminal behavior which is known to you, and (c) protecting confidential information which has come to you as a result of your professional clergy status.

A brief discussion of the resolution of the three cases will conclude the presentation.

Defending One Accused of a Crime

There is little question under Jewish law that a person is not required to plead guilty even if he actually is. This is because in so doing he would waive his right to a trial and such would essentially be the equivalent of requiring him to confess under any and all circumstances. Accordingly, a Jew may (or perhaps even *must*) plead "not guilty" in order to compel the civil authority (Jewish or secular) to prove its case according to the law.[4]

The halakhic scope of a professional's (particularly an attorney's) role in aiding a criminal defendant is established by the Talmudic discussion at *Niddah* 61a which states:

> Raba said: Regarding slander, even though one should not accept its truth, one should nevertheless take note of it. There was a rumor about certain Galileans that they had murdered a person. They came to Rabbi Tarfon and pleaded with him: "Will the Master hide us?" He said to them "But how should I act? If I do not hide you, you will be seen [and summarily executed by the blood avengers.] [On the other hand] if I do hide you the Sages [e.g., Raba, *supra*] have said 'Regarding slander, even though one should not accept its truth, one should nevertheless take note of it [and I would be acting contrary to that ruling].' Go and hide yourselves."

The justification for Rabbi Tarfon's refusal to aid the Galileans remains in dispute among Jewish authorities, which dispute is essential to our understanding of the limitations, if any, upon professional assistance to the guilty.

Rashi flatly states that the reason that Rabbi Tarfon would not help the Galileans was because if they were indeed guilty of murder, his assistance would be prohibited—implying that Jewish law prohibits aiding defendants who might be guilty. But *Tosafot* and Rabbenu Asher *(Rosh)*[5] both disagree, and insist to the

contrary that the justification for Rabbi Tarfon's refusal to help
the Galileans was his fear that the blood avengers would punish
him for assisting in the escape of criminals. Thus his *self-interest* in
personal security justified his refusal to aid the fleeing Galileans.
But *Tosafot* and the *Rosh* both insist that helping them would otherwise be permitted under Jewish law.

The issue for Rashi was Rabbi Tarfon's doubt as to whether or
not the Galileans were actually guilty. This has led one modern
authority to insist that the decision to aid one who is guilty of a
crime depends upon the *actual knowledge of guilt* on the part of the
one whose assistance is requested: "If a lawyer *knows* that his
client has committed a crime, it is forbidden for him to help the
criminal escape the consequences of his act, by relying on some
technical legal points or other devices. The lawyer, just as any
Jew, is directed by the Torah to eradicate the evil from our midst,
and may not actively assist someone to avoid his punishment."[6]

Of course, the practical implications are such that the difference between Rashi and *Tosafot* may not be so great. Criminal
defense attorneys rarely, if ever, *know* their client is guilty because
the establishment of guilt is a legal, and not a factual, conclusion.
A determination of guilt in modern systems of criminal justice
involves the variables of testimony, witnesses, police misconduct
and clearly established criminal intent. We may assume then that
criminal guilt is never really *known* by a professional providing
assistance to an accused defendant.

An interpretation is possible which reconciles Rashi, *Tosafot*
and the *Rosh* and makes no distinction between known guilt and
mere rumors of guilt. This is suggested by understanding Rabbi
Tarfon's hesitation to be essentially out of fear of violating *the secular law* and being punished for said violation. Thus, the sole
limitation on assisting one accused of a crime would be the *danger to one's self*, i.e., will *the secular authorities* chase and appre-
hend you for your assistance?[7]

Modern criminal justice systems not only permit but require
professional assistance to criminal defendants, which is accordingly justified, as well, by Jewish law. If this is correct, then any
form of assistance legally permitted by the secular society and
authority would be permitted under Jewish law.

Particularly in light of current American law[8] this position
appears both logical and sensible: namely that a professional's
assistance simply insures that the secular society is satisfying its

general obligation "to remove evil from its midst," but in the manner in which it has determined is appropriate and just.

Informing the Authorities of Criminal Behavior

A closely connected question to that of defending one accused of a crime is that involving the so-called duty to inform. Again, a classic Talmudic text introduces the problem, from *Baba Metzia* 83b-84a, as follows:

> Rabbi Eleazar, son of Rabbi Simeon, met a police officer, who was arresting thieves. Rabbi Eleazar said to him [the police officer]: "How are you able [to detect] the thieves ... ? Perhaps you take the righteous innocent and leave behind the guilty!" The police officer replied: "But what can I do? It is an order of the [secular] King." [Rabbi Eleazar then attempted to instruct the policeman as to how to determine who was a thief and who was not]·.... The matter was heard in the House of the King. They said: "Let the one who reads the letter be the messenger." Rabbi Eleazar, son of Rabbi Simeon, was then brought to the court and he proceeded to arrest thieves. Rabbi Joshua ben Korchah sent [this message] to him: "Vinegar, son of wine! [You defamer of your father's good name!] How long will you deliver the people of our God for slaughter?" Rabbi Eleazar sent [back] to him: "I am destroying thorns from the vineyard." Rabbi Joshua responded: "Let the owner of the vineyard come and destroy his thorns." ... And also [a similar circumstance to this occurred] to Rabbi Ishmael, the son of Rabbi Jose. The prophet Elijah met him [and] said to him: "How long will you hand over the people of our God for execution?" Rabbi Ishmael responded: "What can I do? It is an order of the King." Elijah retorted: "Your father fled to Asia; you can flee to Laodicea."[9]

So *Baba Metzia* records that two sages of the Gemara were rebuked—one by Rabbi Yehoshua and the other by the prophet Elijah—for assisting the secular government in the prosecution of criminals, suggesting clearly that this conduct is not proper. This position seems clearly to be codified in halakha by *Shulkhan Arukh, Hoshen Mishpat* 488:9, which states: "It is forbidden to denounce a Jew before the gentile authorities, even if he is wicked and a sinner. Anybody who so denounces his fellow Jew forfeits his place in the world to come." But the full and literal import of this clear provision has been nullified, essentially, by its routine interpretation as applying only to turning over a per-

son or his property to the custody of an "oppressor," who inflicts
bodily or financial harm in a manner that is malevolent or
entirely extra-legal.[10]

One line of explanation for Rabbi Joshua's rebuke of Rabbi
Eleazar is that though this conduct (of helping the secular
authorities) was generally permitted, it was deemed inappropriate for the pious and religious leaders of the community. This
understanding is generally based on an inference from the
Jerusalem Talmud, *Terumot* 8:4 as well as the expansion of this
principle by Joseph Karo in *Beit Yosef, Hoshen Mishpat* 388.
According to this analysis, it is only the pious of the community
who are to avoid assisting the secular police and prosecution
authorities, inasmuch as it is undignified and unseemly for this
class to hold themselves out as "assistant policemen"—*though it
is permissible for others* to do so. Following this line of reasoning,
Rabbi Hershel Schachter says: "There is no problem of "*mesirah*"
[informing] the government of the Jewish criminal, even if they
penalize the criminal with a punishment more severely than the
Torah requires, because even a non-Jewish government is authorized to punish and penalize above and beyond the [Jewish] law
… for the purpose of maintaining law and order. However, this
only applies in the situation where the Jewish offender or criminal has violated some Torah law."[11] A fascinating application—
and apparent contradiction—of this principle occurred in a case
involving Rabbi Dr. Moses Tendler, a distinguished professor of
Jewish Law at Yeshiva University as well as the son-in-law of the
late revered halakhic authority Rabbi Moshe Feinstein.

In this case, a convicted murderer appealed his trial conviction on the grounds that his confession of "the brutal stabbing
murder of his twenty-three-year-old pregnant wife" to his regular *shul* rabbi, the esteemed Dr. Tendler, should not have been
admitted at trial. Rabbi Tendler testified against the defendant at
the trial and fully revealed the confession, which resulted in his
conviction. The court determined that "the defendant's communications to Rabbi Tendler were made for the secular purpose of
seeking assistance in the retention of counsel, and in negotiating
with the prosecutor's office and securing other assistance in connection with the preparation of his defense to the charges, and
were not made by the defendant in confidence to Rabbi Tendler
'in his professional character as spiritual advisor.' Accordingly,
the communications were not privileged."[12]

Rabbi Tendler's actions may seem to be in violation of halak-hah if the unenhanced, simple and literal reading of *Shulkhan Arukh, Hoshen Mishpat* 488:9 is used as the standard, and if Rabbi Yehoshua's reprimand of Rabbi Eleazar is understood as restrict-ing the behavior of pious scholars (of whom Rabbi Dr. Moses Tendler would certainly be one). But there is another approach to the text in *Baba Metzia* 83b-84a. This second interpretation rejects the opinion of Rabbi Eleazar and elevates that of Rabbi Joshua to the normative Jewish standard[13]—an opinion which initially prohibits informing the authorities of criminal behavior. If Rabbi Joshua's opinion is normative, then it would be permitted to assist the gentile secular government and its criminal prosecu-tions only when the person poses a threat to others or to the com-munity through his conduct. These situations are based upon the Jewish law of a *rodef*, a pursuer. The law of the *rodef* "not merely permits, but mandates that a bystander come to the rescue of a putative victim whose life is threatened and [even] that, if there is no other way of preserving the life of the intended victim, res-cue be effected by taking the life of the aggressor."[14] Under this reading the dispute between Rabbi Eleazar and Rabbi Joshua takes on a different character.

Rabbi Eleazar can be seen as having come upon an official of the secular authority, the King who is apprehending individuals and delivering them for execution without at all endeavoring to distinguish between the innocent and the guilty. The police offi-cer clearly recognized that his actions were unjust, but pleaded in his defense the doctrine of *force majeure* ("What shall I do? It is the command of the King!"). In all probability, the King in the Talmudic tale was well aware of the fact that arrests were being made indiscriminately, but pursued such a policy because of a desire to instill fear in the hearts of thieves in an effort to cause them to desist from their nefarious conduct. Execution of the innocent was designed either (a) to intimidate those who were indeed criminals or (b) to secure the cooperation of the citizenry, who would themselves bring pressure to bear upon the thieves to desist from their criminal activities. Either way, *de facto*, inno-cent persons were being put to death because of the activities of thieves. Thus, thieves were "pursuers" of the innocent. Since the thieves refused to abandon their criminal activities they were branded as "pursuers" by Rabbi Eleazar who declared that "I am eradicating thorns from the vineyard." The import of that statement may be taken to mean that the criminals were a threat to the innocent just as thorns are a threat to the grapes that would otherwise flourish in the vineyard.

This possibility means that the controversy between Rabbi Eleazar and Rabbi Joshua may well reflect disagreement regarding the level of certainty of impending loss of life that is required to trigger the law of the pursuer—the *rodef*.[15] As is well known, in Jewish law, one who poses a threat to the life of others must be prevented from accomplishing the intended harm. Force—even deadly force—may be used in such a case without the need for a court hearing. And *this threat need not be limited to the possibility that the criminal will actually harm another,* but includes such factors as the possibility that in response to a Jew being apprehended for committing a crime, other Jews will be injured or anti-Semitism will be promoted.[16]

Indeed Rashi argues elsewhere that Jewish law recognizes that a secular government may properly enforce any law validly promulgated under the rule "the law of the land is the law" (*dina de-malkhuta dina*), even against Jews.[17] The policy value of the application of this principle is "maintaining law and order"[18] or "the prevention of the world's destruction."[19] And it was pursuant to such an argument that Rabbi Moshe Feinstein allowed a Jew to serve as a tax auditor for the United States Government, in a situation wherein the audit might result in the criminal prosecution of Jews for evading taxes.[20]

The dispute in *Baba Metzia* 83b-84a may thus be summarized: many authorities rule that only those viewed as of exemplary piety must avoid assisting in the prosecution of Jewish criminals providing that the criminal prosecution is for conduct that violates Jewish law but otherwise there are no obstacles to others assisting in criminal prosecutions. Others disagree and follow Rabbi Joshua holding that it is prohibited to assist the secular government in criminal prosecutions unless the criminal poses a general danger to society (the *rodef*). In practical application, the result may indeed be the same.

Professional Confidence

There can be no question that though Judaism places strong and severe restrictions upon disclosure of confidential information,[21]

Jewish law also requires one to inform a Jew of harm that might befall him and which could be avoided.[22] This tension reflects the conflict inherent in Leviticus 19:16, between its two provisions (a) "thou shall not go about as a bearer of tales among your people"[23] and (b) "do not stand by while your brother's blood is being shed." Though the stricture against disclosure of confidential information results in a moral code "even more restricted in some respects than presently accepted canons of professional confidentiality,"[24] the countervailing obligation to help others and divulge secrets for that purpose applies not only to saving lives but also to preventing monetary loss.[25] It is understood by contemporary halakhic authorities that no person has the right to divulge information of a personal nature concerning a fellow man or woman simply to satisfy the curiosity of a third party. The crucial consideration is thus the "need to know" in the sense of avoiding potential harm.[26] Respect for privacy and the inviolability of the professional relationship certainly do not take precedence over the protection of the lives and safety of others. This latter consideration is of sufficient weight to oblige a physician, attorney or member of the clergy to take whatever measures may be necessary to eliminate the danger. If, however, no danger exists or *if the danger can be averted by other means* , he may not violate the confidence. The desire to see an evil doer brought to justice and punished for his crime is not, in itself, sufficient reason to justify a breach of confidence.[27] It is clear that a cloak of strict confidentiality ordinarily obtains in any discussion that a rabbi has with a member of his or her congregation. Its breach can only be justified, according to Jewish law, in circumstances in which lives or money will be saved and "the prevention of the destruction of the world"[28] will be advanced.

Conclusion

Modern rabbis face a delicate dilemma in circumstances in which criminal behavior is disclosed to them during the course of their professional responsibilities. In addition to the presumption of confidentiality regarding any communication given to a rabbi, there is the question of the rabbi's a priori relationship to secular authority. In no instance does Jewish law suggest that a rabbi is an agent or assistant to the police or prosecuting authorities. Such assistance (as in the case of Rabbi Eleazar in *Baba Metzia* 83b-84a), must find specific justification from among a system of values which places life and the maintenance of law and order at its apex. Such justification depends upon the relative weights which the rabbinic personality places on these various policy considerations.

In the cases outlined at the beginning of this paper, no reference to secular authority was made by the rabbi. Following pastoral counseling, the scheme to harbor an illegal alien was voluntarily terminated. The real estate and bank fraud was the subject of an indictment and plea of guilty, and the abusive parent was convinced to obtain counseling and treatment which resulted in the end of misbehavior a restored standard of appropriate conduct.

In assessing the degree to which we should hasten to assist the guilty or "turn them in," an obvious and central philosophical question for the modern rabbi concerns the appropriate and justified degree of confidence in secular authority. Classical rabbinic Judaism exhibited a strong distrust of secular authority. Though we surely live in a different world, "calling the police" may nevertheless best remain a last and desperate resort.

Notes

1. Temple Sinai of Sharon is a 550 family congregation in Sharon, Massachusetts, a south suburb of Boston.
2. For obvious reasons the names of the individuals involved will not be used nor divulged. In addition, the relevant statutes of limitations applicable for the commission of the crimes to which reference is herein made have all run, thus vitiating the criminal culpability and legal vulnerability which may have otherwise obtained.
3. The actual resolution of the three cases will be addressed at the end of the paper.
4. Maimonides, *Sanhedrin* 18:6; see generally J. David Bleich, *Contemporary Halakhic Problems* II (New York: 1983), pp. 349-357 and Norman Lamm, *Faith and Doubt* (New York: 1986), pp. 78-92 .
5. *Tosafot, Niddah* 61a (s.v. *"atmarinkhu"*) and Rabbenu Asher, *Tosafot Harosh* on Niddah 61a (s.v. *"atmarinkhu"*).
6. Hershel Schachter, *"Dina Di'Malchusa Dina*: Secular Law as a Religious Obligation," *Journal of Halacha and Contemporary Society* 103, 121-22 (Spring

1981), citing Rabbi Shelomo Luria, *Hokhmat Shelomo,* commenting on Niddah 61a; and Rabbi Akiva Eiger on Niddah 61a [emphasis mine].

7. This is advanced by Michael J. Broyde, *The Pursuit of Justice and Jewish Law* (New York: 1996) p. 94, citing Rabbi Yaakov Ettlinger, *Arukh Laner,* commenting on Niddah 61a, Rabbi Yaakov Emden, *She'elat Ya'avetz* 2:9, and Rabbi Moshe Shreiber, *Hatam Sofer* 6:14.

8. See, e.g., Nix v. Whiteside, 475 U.S. 157 (1986) (a United States Supreme Court decision ruling that though a lawyer may, as most states require that he must, inform the court of perjury by his client there are circumstances in which one has the "right" to present a false case in order to compel the government to prove its accusations beyond a reasonable doubt).

9. The Gemara's reference is to the Roman province of Asia, *Asia Proconsularis,* to which Jews fled in order to avoid public appointment under the authority of the Roman Empire. Elijah's statement thus seems to suggest a rebuke along the lines of: "Your father had the courage to resist the pressure of secular authority; if you were a worthy son, you would show the same character."

10. David J. Bleich, "Jewish Law and the State's Authority to Punish Crime," 12 *Cardozo Law Review,* 829, 830 (1991).

11. Hershel Schachter "*Dina Di'Malchusa Dina*: Secular Law as a Religious Obligation," pp. 103, 118.

12. People v. Drelich, 506 N.Y.S. 2d 746, 124 A.D. 2d 441 (2d App. Div. 1986).

13. There are a number of authorities whose inferences suggest such an approach: Maimonides, *Hilchot Rotzeah* 2:4; *Tosafot* to *Sanhedrin* 20b; see generally David J. Bleich, "Jewish Law and the State's Authority to Punish Crime," 12 *Cardozo L aw Review* 829, 840-44 (1991).

14. J. David Bleich, "Jewish Law and the State's Authority to Punish Crime," 12 *Cardoza Law Review* 829, 849 (1991).

15. Ibid., 849-50.

16. These principles are applied in a famous commentary of Rabbi Moses Isserles (the *Rama)* which rules that a Jew who engages in counterfeiting or the like may be turned over to civil authorities for punishment. *Rama* commenting on *Shulkhan Arukh, Hoshen Mishpat* 388:12, 425:1.

17. *Rashi* commenting on Gittin 9b (s.v. *dinim).*

18. Michael J. Broyde, *The Pursuit of Justice and Jewish Law* (New York: 1996), p. 87.

19. Maimonides, *Hilchot Melachim* 10:11 (*shelo yishacheit ha-olam*) suggests a natural law theory of Jewish obligation to the secular world which would justify a very expansive reading of the otherwise routinely constricted understanding of *dina de-malkhuta dina* in Jewish law. The full quote from Maimonides' *Mishneh Torah* is as follows: "The *Beit Din* of Israel is obligated to establish judges for these resident aliens to judge them in accordance with these laws *in order that the world not be destroyed.* If the *Beit Din* sees fit to appoint judges from among them, they may do so; and if they see fit to appoint Jewish judges for them, they may do so." [emphasis mine]

See generally Gil Graff, " *Separation of Church and State: Dina de'Malchuta Dina," Jewish Law, 1750-1848* (University, Alabama: 1985*).* The standard Talmudic references to *dina demalchuta dina* are found in Gittin 10b; Baba Kamma 113a; Baba Batra 54b; and Nedarim 28a.

The argument advanced, has been that state statutes which mandate clergy disclosure and breach of confidentiality in cases of child abuse should be honored and observed under the rubric of *dina d'malchuta dina*. I do not agree. If child abuse is observed or suspected from information obtained outside the bounds of a confidential rabbi/congregant relationship, then such information may and should be reported to secular and civil authorities pursuant to general principles of Jewish law apart from any applicable state statute. If, however, the knowledge is obtained in the context of a confidential relationship, its confidential character and the constraints placed by Jewish law upon its breach mandate, in my opinion, its protection and the rabbi's refusal to disclose. Even in cases of extreme urgency, circumstances in which direct observation of a putative victim is possible by a rabbi or other synagogue professional, confidentiality is preferred not the breach of professional clergy confidentiality. *Dina d'malchuta dina* is not understood by Jewish tradition to be an all-emcompassing and ever-elastic standard which incorporates any block of secular law as binding and valid. When it conflicts directly with standards of Jewish law (as, I argue, here) its value must be weighed against the value of the countervailing principles of Jewish law then in contention.

20. Moshe Feinstein, *Iggerot Mosheh, Hoshen Mishpat* 1:92.
21. Maimonides, *Hilkhot De'ot* 7:2; Yoma 4b.
22. Michael J. Broyde, *The Pursuit of Justice and Jewish Law* (New York: 1996) p. 25.
23. Other *halakhic* concerns involve the avoidance of the negative *mitzvot* of *lashon hara* and *lo tailaich rachil*. *See* Cohen, Rabbi Alfred S., "On Maintaining A Professional Confidence," 7 *Journal of Halacha and Contemporary Society* 73,77 (1984); Cohen, Rabbi Alfred S., "Privacy: A Jewish Perspective," *Journal of Halacha and Contemporary Society* 53, 82-87 (1981) and authorities cited therein.
24. J. David Bleich, *Contemporary Halakhic Problems* II (New York: 1983) p. 75. For an excellent and continuously updated summary of the state of American law regarding professional clergy confidentiality, *see* Annot., Matters to Which the Privilege Covering Communication to Clergymen or Spiritual Advisors Extends, 71 ALR3d 794 (1976).
25. Hofetz Hayim, *Be'er Mayim Hayim, Hilkhot Issurei Rekhilut* 9:1. See Aaron Kirschenbaum, "The Bystander's Duty to Rescue in Jewish Law," 8 *Journal of Religious Ethics* 204-226 (1980).
26. J. David Bleich, *Contemporary Halakhic Problems* II (New York: 1983), p. 76.
27. Ibid., p. 78.
28. See footnote 19, *supra*.

Chapter 4

❖   ❖   ❖

PUNISHMENT
Its Method and Purpose

Walter Jacob

All legal systems need a way of enforcing court decisions; punishment represents one of those means. It may be provided to exact or to circumvent vengeance, to rehabilitate, educate, enforce social norms, maintain class distinctions, exercise power, or for a variety of other reasons. Jewish law also used different methods of enforcement. The reasoning behind them may be clearly stated or implicit.

Effectiveness demanded a system of readily understood punishments and penalties governed by a rationale readily understood by the offender, the injured party, the surviving family, and the broader society. Various periods of Jewish history have seen the judiciary take different paths. The punishments provided rarely indicated the intent of those who imposed it and there was no extended debate of what punishment sought to accomplish. Occasional hints may point to some general theories of punishment. We shall investigate what punishments were used as well as those avoided. In other words, not only the paths taken, but the road eschewed. Punishment for social or religious violations have changed several times since the biblical period, but not necessarily in the direction which we ascribe to it. This paper will present only a skeletal outline with some tentative conclusions.[1] The subject is immense and so this essay can only begin to explore it.

Judaism since Biblical times has defined itself through a system of *mitzvot*—commandments. These are not suggestions, but divine demands on human conduct. They were worded very clearly, with "You shall" or "you shall not," as in the Decalogue and elsewhere,[2] dealt with specific situations as in many laws of Exodus and Leviticus.They might begin "If a person ...," and then conclude with a penalty which may simply be a fine or go as far as demanding death,[3] or they might be presented as actual cases.

As the commandments were to be taken seriously, a system of timely penalties and punishments accompanied them. Some punishments were mentioned in the Decalogue, but far fewer than we might have expected and their nature did not make them socially useful. How would the average rogue react to the penalties provided by the Decalogue—"I will not hold him guiltless" or "visit the sins of the fathers upon the children for the third and fourth generation" or "will prolong their days in the land which the Lord your God will give you?" These specifics were not translatable into daily life unless the individual was truly religious. Furthermore no penalties were attached to the most common breaches of family and social morality mentioned by the Decalogue—murder, robbery, and adultery. Punishments were, however, provided later in the Torah.

What was the goal of the Torah's legal system? Exodus declared that Israel was to become "a kingdom of priests, a holy people" and that was reiterated in Deuteronomy as well as later. The thought was shared throughout the long biblical period.[4] In other words a special status of sanctity was to be achieved by the entire people. Whatever else holiness might mean, it certainly demanded the elimination of sin, as well as personal and social misconduct. The lofty goal was left undefined, but sins toward God and human beings were delineated and enumerated. The Torah, as a religious document, treated religious and ritual wrong-doings alongside crimes against individuals and society.

As the Torah is a religious document, not a national legal code, it would have been appropriate to leave punishments to God.

Divine punishment could be meted out in the form of diseases, accidents, farming or business misfortunes, and might be delivered in this or succeeding generations. The entire natural and human world could be seen as enforcing agencies. Punishment could also be postponed to the next world with powerful descriptions of the site of such punishment, as vivid as Dante's Hell. Judaism sometimes took the first path and interpreted disasters of a personal nature as punishment for specific acts[5] or national disasters as divine punishment for wrong doing of the entire people. Such an interpretation was frequently invoked[6] and continued to be used as an explanation for great national disasters such as the destruction of the Temple, the expulsion from Spain, and the Holocaust.[7] These explanations usually served best in a hortatory setting.

The religious goal was the creation of a "holy nation." Social goals also emerge from the legislation and its provisions for punishment. Let us begin with the most serious offenses, murder and manslaughter, which although rare, arouse strong emotions, we will then turn to other crimes.

The biblical legislation sought to prevent human vengeance and to channel matters into the hands of the law. Murder was differentiated from accidental killing and so were the punishments. The cities of refuge provided a safe haven for the innocent,[8] although we know nothing about the way in which they functioned, and they were not replicated in any form in later Jewish history. Murder was severely punished through the death penalty, which was carried out by the courts or by the relatives of the victim, so Cain in Genesis was free to be killed by anyone who felt that the blood of Abel needed to be avenged.[9] This citation came from an era in which the court system was not sufficiently strong to carry out penalties and this method of justice was condemned.[10] Blasphemy also carried the death penalty, as did misappropriation of divine property (i.e. something declared *herem*).[11] The death penalty was invoked for many crimes, though not for crimes against property as in many non-Jewish jurisdictions until the nineteenth century.[12] Executions were carried out through various means with stoning used most frequently, followed by fire. Hanging was not a method of execution although a corpse might have been hung in order to shame the individual or to warn others.[13]

The death penalty could be invoked against an entire community if it was involved in apostasy;[14] the city was then totally destroyed. We may be astonished by the constant use of the death penalty; justice was severe.

With the suspected adulteress *(sotah)*, the trial by ordeal was as frightening, as the punishment could be death, at the husband's discretion.[15] In this case, we also have a public spectacle of a highly dramatic nature, as we learn especially from the tractate by that name in the Babylonian Talmud, which detailed the proceedings before the court.

Young women about to enter marriage were especially vulnerable to charges of non-virginity, so the punishment for a false accusation was severe and consisted of a fine of one hundred shekels, whipping, and the inability to ever divorce his wife. The same penalty was provided for someone who raped a girl who was not betrothed; if she was, the penalty was death, [16] strange to our ears indeed.

A system of precise retribution, aside from vengeance for murder, discussed earlier, was provided by the statements "An eye for an eye" which demanded monetary compensation through the courts.[17] A slave was given freedom if seriously injured by his master.[18] These laws protected the perpetrator from personal vengeance and allowed the facts to be investigated. A harsh punishment, however, was decreed for a woman who sought to assist her husband during a fight by seizing the genitals of his opponent; her hand is cut off.[19]

Whipping was frequently invoked, although mentioned specifically only once, it seems to have been taken for granted as it was mentioned without a specific offense, but as a general punishment. It was considered disciplinary in nature. It seems to have been frequently used to discipline slaves. [20]

Some punishments were intended to make crime expensive, so the system of high fines in addition to restitution were invoked and should have made the potential thief think twice about his actions (seven fold or five fold for an ox, four fold for a sheep).[21] Even an innocent purchaser, who presumably did not investigate the source of his purchase sufficiently, paid a two fold penalty.[22] Theft voluntarily acknowledged brought restitution and the addition of a fifth of the value, plus a guilt offering.[23] Many laws dealt with the protection of property, although we should note that the notion of personal possession was limited by the laws of the Sabbatical Year and the Jubilee.[24] The latter was theoretical, but the Book of Jubilees testified to a desire to follow it.

Imprisonment was used only for holding a suspect until trial, for political reasons, or to enforce a judicial decision. It was not generally used as a method of punishment.[25] Confiscation was mentioned only at the end of the biblical period.[26]

The laws sought to protect the weak and demanded a fair judicial system which treated all persons regardless of status alike. This included the non-Israelite stranger and the slave.[27]

There are, of course, instances when no human punishment is possible as the commandment deals with a matter of conscience alone, such as the tenth commandment. Who knows when "You shall not covet" .... has been violated? We must leave this to God and the human conscience.

The Bible was not the product of systematic thinkers. We, therefore, have no theoretical statements about the function of punishment whether carried out by divine mandate or through human agency. We must deduce what we can from isolated statements and various hints.

The human court carried out a divine mandate, so the punishment was seen as ultimately coming from God to help to produce a "holy nation." Punishment played a social role as it generally was public; the people participated or were required to participate, so that the communal nature of this final stage of a trial was likely to have an impressive religious effect and may have been planned as a deterrent as well. The court's intervention took punishment out of the realm of personal vengeance and replaced it with communal action. It was also a display of royal, priestly, or communal power and protected that power and its system of courts. For the individual, the prospect of public humiliation before the entire community played a significant role.

The Mishnah and the Two Talmuds

The Mishnah and the two Talmuds vastly expanded the range of law. Many of the areas covered must have existed earlier because a society could hardly have functioned with the skeletal system of the Torah, but we possess no record of that coverage. The Mishnah and the Jerusalem and Babylonian Talmuds present detailed discussions, actual cases, and academic analyses of problems. Often it is difficult to distinguish among them. Matters which were no longer actual, as those connected with the Temple and its ritual as well as the "King's Law" were debated.[28] A series of hermeneutical rules, interpreting and expanding the original biblical material were carefully developed.[29] These rules tied the "oral law" to the earlier "written law" and provided a justification for the expansion. The judiciary was fleshed out and various levels of courts which may also have existed earlier, but were not described in the Bible, were mentioned.

Punishments for crimes were also changed, and in some instances, expanded or reinterpreted. Whipping, for example, was seen as a merciful act, as any trespass against a divine commandment actually deserved the death penalty.[30] An entire mishnaic tractate bore the name "Lashes," although it also contained discussions of other material. The number of lashes was diminished to thirty-nine to avoid a possible mistake and then could be further reduced for medical reasons or to spare the honor of the person to be punished.[31] On the other hand, if the individual died during the administration of the whip, no one was blamed. Its administration was also described in detail; three judges had to be present during its administration.[32] The specific crimes for which whipping was the penalty were detailed; they included all offenses for which *karet* was the biblical penalty as well as all violations of a negative commandment which entailed some action, so tale-bearing, prohibited in Leviticus 19:14, would not lead to whipping. On the other hand taking the name of God in vain was so punished.[33] This form of punishment was also extended to provide communal discipline, so those who made impossible vows were flogged as were individuals who had intercourse in public, or a man and a woman who secluded themselves.[34] The limit of thirty-nine lashes only existed for offenses against negative commandments, there was no limit for positive commandments. Therefore, if the command to build a sukkah was met by refusal, the individual could be whipped, as could a debtor.[35] We shall see this form of punishment vastly expanded as a disciplinary measure in later times.

Confiscation, hardly mentioned in the Bible, was extended and meant that the courts could punish far beyond the fines provided by the Scripture this was used particularly to punish repeating offenders, as a means of restoring law and order,[36] or to provide what common sense demanded, but for which no other precedent existed, such as the sale of an infant's property for the seller's own benefit or invalidating a marriage which had been legally executed.[37] It was also used to justify Hillel's *prosbul*, in other words to justify a quasi-legislative act of social reform.[38] The system of fines was expanded to cover numerous situations; they were often fixed by law so that equity was assured. There was some disagreement whether fines earlier imposed only by a *bet din* could be continued, but there was consensus on the power of the court to fine for any matter not covered by biblical law.[39]

The death penalty and the methods of execution were discussed in detail. Four methods of execution were used: stoning, burning, strangulation, and decapitation.[40] Each of these methods of execution was arranged in such a way that the convicted individual's physical appearance would not change. The thought behind this was that of making the execution resemble a normal death as much as possible with the body of the criminal left unmutilated.[41] This was considered an extension of the commandment to love your neighbor as yourself and assured a humane death.[42] These two considerations continue the biblical thought of having the court act as an agent of the Divine and following that pattern as much as possible.

Stoning, the penalty for eighteen Biblically mentioned crimes, was changed so that the criminal was pushed from a height onto stones, rather than having stones thrown at him. The general public was also effectively excluded and only the witnesses took part.[43] Burning, for adultery and incest, was preceded by strangulation.[44] Decapitation, prescribed principally for murder, followed the Roman practice.[45] Strangulation was used for all crimes in which no other death penalty was specified; it was considered the most humane method of execution.[46] Safeguards against wrongful execution were carefully put into place.[47] Following stoning the corpse could be hanged for public display until nightfall if the crime was blasphemy or idolatry.[48] As these executions were painful, a drug potion including frankincense was given to them.[49]

Although theoretically the death penalty was not to be extended beyond the instances mentioned in the Torah, in practice this was not so.[50] Some efforts were made to limit the use of the death penalty. It seems that during portions of the late mishnaic period it disappeared entirely or was so infrequent that it no longer played a role, so one authority stated that a court which gave the death sentence once in seven years was a bad court, while Eliezer b. Azaria increased that to once in seventy years. R. Tarfon and R. Akiba would not impose the death penalty at all.

The talmudic discussion suggested that the penalty be avoided by asking questions of the witnesses till some confusion arose.[51]

These brief statements against the death penalty, as well as others which sought to void it in the case of the rebellious son, do not change the basic tenor of the talmudic discussion. The death penalty remained part of the legal system and could be used when jurisdiction was provided.

The use of imprisonment was expanded and we learn of separate prisons for Jews and non-Jews.[52] It continued to be used to hold suspects for trial and convicted criminals until their punishment. It was also used to force individuals to obey the will of the court.[53] Furthermore, it was used to sentence a murderer who could not be convicted for technical reasons and for repeat offenders who were not discouraged by whipping. Such prisoners could be fed bread and bad water or barley water, which would lead to their death.[54]

The effort of this literature to clearly delineate the rights and prerogatives of various courts collapsed when the original system of ordination upon which all of this was based vanished. This occurred in the third or fourth century.[55] The literature took it for granted that the authority of the court remained intact despite the lack of ordination. Theoretically, the death penalty was no longer possible, but it continued to be used.

As we look at the Babylonian and Jerusalem Talmud from the point of view of punishment and punitive theory, we see that both added an enormous amount of detail which we have made no attempt to present here. For every biblical law there are dozens of cases, exceptions, peripheral elements, objections both real and theoretical. In addition, the crimes covered were increased as the Biblical laws were too skeletal and because the civilization or the country in which the people now lived had changed. New social and economic conditions had to be met. The basic types of punishment remained the same. Capital punishment may have diminished, but that is far from certain, and it was not eliminated.

Fines were a method of punishment expanded by the Talmud; they went beyond compensation for damage actually suffered. In most cases the amount of the fine was fixed by law and meant that a system was created.[56] Fines could be imposed for many crimes and a very long list existed. Even when the legal right to impose a fine was weak, it could be upheld through custom and the need of the time.[57]

The laws of robbery and theft followed the biblical statements closely; the discussions presented considerable detail as
well as actual cases, but made few basic changes.[58]

The ban *(herem)* was changed from its biblical connotation of
complete destruction or dedication to God; in the Bible it was not
a method of punishment except through a threat made by Ezra.[59]
The Mishnah introduced the *nidui* which was a lesser form of the
herem, but saw it as punishment through isolation; the biblical
basis for this was found in the Book of Numbers.[60] It was used to
punish both scholars and laymen during the Tanaitic period.[61]
Nidui seems usually to have been for a period of thirty days
which might be extended for an additional term. If compliance
was not achieved, then *herem* could be pronounced and it was
effective until lifted by the court. A shorter period of imposed
isolation was the *nezifah* with a duration of only seven days.[62]
The forms of isolation differed in their severity, i.e. whether
study or business was permitted, and whether there were restrictions on washing, clothing, public greeting, participation in public worship or *mezuman*, as well as funerary dishonor.[63] A long
series of offenses could be punished by *nidui*.[64]

In the vast talmudic literature we will not find much theoretical discussion of punishment or the development of penal theory. The various penalties were to punish for crimes, to serve as
deterrents to prospective criminals, and to maintain social order.
The range of application had widened considerably beyond that
of the biblical period, but that may be more apparent than real, for
our knowledge of biblical punishment is very limited.

In contrast to the Bible, there was discussion among the
authorities about the punishment used and the manner of its
execution. Authorities who disagreed and provided other penalties were cited, even if not with approval. We, therefore, see a
diversity of courts emerge in these centuries.

Post-Talmudic Halakhic Authority

At the conclusion of the talmudic period, the court system of the
previous age survived in the Gaonate which continued to exercise
considerable authority in the Near East and the southern Medi-
terranean basin during the early Islamic period of the Umayad
(661-750) and Abbasid (750-1100) caliphates. When the Abbasid

Empire disintegrated, local authorities in various lands assumed judicial authority as they had earlier in Southern and Central Europe. As local rulers were generally quite willing to permit internal autonomy to the Jewish communities, the system of courts and their sentences followed the talmudic pattern with amplification as needed.

As the earlier talmudic law had frequently gone beyond the "written law" with only a slender scriptural connection, so the post-talmudic courts found ways to expand the "oral law" when the need arose. Often steps taken as temporary measures became permanent. The Tanaim had already made a modification by allowing the selection of lay judges by the litigants; the Amoraim went further, so that a single "expert" could adjudicate. Now decision in monetary matters would be made by judges who did not possess the ancient ordination which ceased in the fourth century.

Whipping and the death penalty were theoretically limited, but continued.[65] A new series of punishments was imposed through *takkanot* (communal decrees), often intended only as temporary, but they usually became permanent. Legislation established by a city or provincial assembly of scholars as well as individual decisions of local rabbis were to be obeyed because "of the needs of the time" and this could and did lead to a long list of penalties.[66]

These changes also influenced punishments which often were dictated by the need to protect the community. The ancient requirements as modified in the rabbinic literature made it very difficult to convict anyone as the laws of evidence often required specific warnings or precise corroboration; they did, however, truly protect the individual. Much of this was part of a general medieval need for solidarity in the face of a hostile world and the emphasis on the society rather than the individual.

On the other hand, some types of punishment disappeared entirely, for example the ordeal of the *sotah*, was not mentioned again. Even trial by ordeal was quite common among neighboring cultures in the medieval period, it was not found among Jews.

The death penalty which continued during the talmudic period, despite occasional objections, was fully enforced, except in the Gaonic period and it was used for new situations, for example on informers who were a danger to the entire community; the struggle against them was considered a war to be waged without mercy. The ordinary murderer was also executed as earlier. Executions were by strangulation or drowning, and also sometimes held secretly.[67]

The justification for its use was the removal of evil from the community. Others saw it as a way of frightening potential criminals. Often the right to execute had to be authorized by the local ruler or the king. There is no way of knowing how frequently the death penalty was used. Our sources deal primarily with the best known scholars; they refer to this sentence as nothing unusual. We should remember that the medieval period was much more violent than our times in urban areas and on the roads, as contemporary non-Jewish sources attest.

Added to the list of punishments was maiming, which was unknown in biblical or talmudic times. It was used in both Spain and Poland for a variety of crimes, a habitual Polish thief had both ears cut off. As one respondent indicated, this was more feared than death, as it was a reminder to the world of criminal acts for the rest of the individual's life.[68]

Prisons were used in the Middle Ages in all lands except France and Germany. In Spain imprisonment occurred only for serious crimes such as murder. We even have an inquiry about the need for a *mezuzah* for a prison. House arrest with a guard posted outside the house was also used, especially in Spain.[69]

A method of punishment influenced by the surrounding society was the placement of offenders into iron stocks before the entrance of main synagogue as in Lvov and other Polish cities, a procedure known to us through the *pinkasim* (communal records) of the cities.[70] Another unusual penalty was branding the letter *tav* for prostitution, theft, and/or informing as reported from Spain, Prague, and Cracow.[71] Equally shaming was the shaving of all hair and the beard; this was not known in Gaonic times, but was later used in all lands.[72]

Whipping was the most frequent physical punishment. Maimonides provided a long and detailed list of crimes for which whipping was the punishment; twenty-one were crimes against communal morality in which the Torah stipulated *karet*, a divine punishment of unknown meaning, but not death; eighteen dealt with priestly wrongs and matters connected with sacrifices; 168 covered everything from slander and perjury to dietery and sumptuary laws. This was a much more thorough list than presented by anyone earlier.[73] The medieval punishment of lashes was not governed by the earlier rules which limited it to forty, and the Mishnah diminished to thirty-nine; whippings went far beyond that. It could be part of a system of penance and lead to consecutive whippings.[74] Sometimes it was used as a means of execution. This bodily punishment also led to public shame and so was quite effective.[75]

Whipping and fines were not limited to crimes against individuals, but were also used to punish infringements of a religious nature. In other words, punishment was a tool used to uphold communal morality in a broad sense. Violation of the Sabbath and inappropriate behavior on holidays was punished. In some places individuals could be whipped publicly for a minor infringement such as lighting a fire or a candle after Shabbat had officially begun, or for the more the major offense of not attending public services to provide a *minyan*. In this way a minimum set of religious observances was enforced.[76]

The least problematic form of punishment were fines, and we find them frequently in the responsa literature used for situations not mentioned earlier. Some were quite serious as (accepting stolen goods) and others trivial, as (bringing a dog to synagogue).[77] Unlike previous ages, fines were generally not paid to the injured party, but to the communal treasury and used for a charitable cause. In some instances, the injured party could stipulate the recipient charity.[78] When jurisdiction was provided by the gentile government. It was often stipulated that a portion of all fines collected would be paid into its treasury.

The *herem* in its various forms was used in the medieval period not only as punishment, but as a threat of punishment. For example, and so it was attached to the decree attributed to R. Gershom which prohibited polygamy. The conditions of the *herem* were made more severe, so that it affected the entire family; the wife and children were excluded from synagogue and school. Circumcision and burial would not be performed. The individual and his family were treated as if they did not exist. Within the closed Jewish communities, this was a severe and effective punishment.[79]

This form of punishment ceased to be effective by the nineteenth century when it was used too freely in the struggle between *mitnagdim* and Hassidim as well as the battle between Orthodoxy and the Reform movement. When used nowadays by the extreme Orthodox, it is more a sign of their anger than an effective tool. The collapse of a united community meant it was no longer useful even when properly applied. The same was true of penance which ceased to be mentioned in the responsa literature. The communal base for such actions diminished further and further.

Forms of penance as a path to reconciliation with God had their roots in the Bible with its system of guilt and atonement offerings as well as fasting. They were stipulated, but not legally enforced as this was an area between God and the individual. They could be used as a form of punishment. The Talmud developed them, but not in the direction of a court directed punishment as was the case in the Middle Ages. Whipping, shaving of the head and beard, and fasting along with financial restitution was imposed.[80]

Aside from the traditional uses of punishment of earlier periods to control criminal behavior, the medieval authorities utilized it as a way of enforcing communal discipline. As the world around them was often hostile, strict discipline was necessary to hold the community together. The threat of punishment should therefore be seen as preventive or educational. The methods used reflected the general standards of the times, so new and cruel methods, not previously found, were introduced. There were limits beyond which the punishment could not go for the possiblity of simply leaving the Jewish community always existed. So a balance between reinforcing communal discipline and forcing a member out of the community had to be found.[81] No general theories of punishment were developed and none of the medieval philosophers treated this area.

Conclusions

As we look over the punishments used through the centuries, we see that a number of different goals were sought: (a) The execution of the Divine will; (b) the establishment of a "holy people" with high ideals which would lead to the Messianic Age; (c) the removal of evil from the midst of the people; (d) the elimination of personal vengeance; (e) the prevention of evil through a fear of punishment; (f) the re-education of the criminal; (g) the maintenance of limited autonomy in the face of gentile power; (h) the preservation of the community and its integrity and (i) the elimination of dissidence.

Although each of these forms of punishment used were primarily applied to the individual found guilty, in the medieval period they were applied to the family through various forms of the ban. Many questioned this broader application of punishment and its effect; however, the practical consideration of its effectiveness in difficult times led to its intermittent use.

The considerations here mentioned were used as justification for punishment throughout our long history. They vary from the ideal to the highly utilitarian; as one looks at the literature and the authorities who mention these justifications, we see that the nature of the times and the nature of the personalities played a major role in determining which rationale was emphasized. The talmudic authorities and their later medieval successors rarely present us with any discussion of a theory of punishment or with a listing of alternative rationales. In fact in most instances when a rationale has been given at all, it was incidental to the punishment. Only when asked whether the sentence would have an adverse affect on the community or the individual was a rationale presented at all. Those who made the decisions were more interested in the task of practical leadership for their community than in a theory of criminology. Those who wrote codes wished to present a concise synopsis of the vast fields of the halakhah and, with the exception of Maimonides, added little theoretical material to their volumes. The great debates about the nature and purpose of punishment at human hands existed only in rudimentary forms.

The biblical efforts were intended to remove punishment from the hands of the individual through a system of courts and this succeeded. The courts and the law which accompanied them took care of all disputes. Both were firmly established; the power and authority of the halakhah, became firmly rooted, so that anarchy never reigned even in the worst of times. This was relatively easy in periods of independence or when a high degree of autonomy was given to the Jewish community and, to a lesser degree, in ages when submission to the will of the courts was voluntary. The punishments, of course, had to be tailored to the conditions which prevailed.

Human punishment through courts dampened the desire for vengeance. We see this especially with the treatment of murder and physical injury. Equally important, it leveled the ground between the powerful and well-connected and the ordinary human being. Justice, ultimately, in the hands of God, could be found in the courts and was mete out according to the crime and the facts, not personal status. Humaneness in the nature of the punishment was a goal sought as well. In the Bible we see it through leaving many punishments in the hands of God, by the establishment of the cities of refuge, a system of fines, etc. The trend toward a more humane system was accelerated in the rabbinic period when we find the death penalty, so frequently invoked in the Bible, much more limited. Execution occurred mainly for murder and was performed in a less painful manner and with the general population effectively excluded. Efforts were also made to limit whipping and to take the physical condition of the individual sentenced into account. Often fines could be substituted for physical punishment.

The medieval period accepted the rabbinic modifications in the Mishnah and the Talmud, but often moved in the direction of severity in accordance with the perceived needs of the times. The jurisdiction to impose punishments was extended as necessary and at times the methods used by the surrounding society were used. They were not sufficiently frequent to arouse objection or discussion. Although thousands of responsa deal with every facet of human life, only a fraction of them mention punishments. It is, therefore, difficult to assess the frequency of the imposition of any punishment.

As we follow the pattern of punishment through the ages, we must be keenly aware that change occurred readily and frequently. It went far beyond using the methods of the surrounding world. Judaism displayed a constant resilience and ability to make radical changes when it was necessary. The clearest example is the creation of a new system of judges and courts after rabbinic ordination had disappeared. This was done in keeping with the spirit of tradition, but existed entirely outside its parameters.

Studies of punishment in Jewish law, as so in so many other areas need to be carried out in depth with evidence from the legal literature augmented by other sources, both Jewish and gentile. Such studies will carry their share of surprises as, perhaps, this study.

Notes

1. A very extensive bibliography, especially of the Hebrew literature has been provided by Nahum Rakover, *Otzar Hamishpat*, Vol. 1 (Jerusalem: 1975), pp. 271-302; Vol. 2 (Jerusalem: 1992), pp. 263-301. Many publications are not readily accessible. The bibliography could be annotated to note essays which are traditional and non-historic in their approach, those which are apologetic, those which seek to apply the tradition to modern Israel, etc.

2. Ex. 20; Deut. 5, Lev. 18, 19, Deut. 22

3. Ex. 21 and 22, Lev. 5, etc.

4. Ex. 19.5; Deut. 7.6, 14.2, 21; 26,19; 28.9; Is. 62.12; Dan. 8.24; 12.7

5. For taking divine property—1 Sam 15.1-33, divine anger is incurred; cursing God punished by God, Lev 24.15; sexual relations with a brother's wife leads to childlessness, Ex 20.21; various sexual offenses will be divinely punished, Ex 20.17ff.; homosexuality Lev 20.13; a series of curses for a wide variety of offenses sexual, familial, and social, Deut 27.15-26.

6. When booty declared as *herem* was taken, the entire people were punished through defeat, Josh 6.17; 7.1-12; apostasy on the part of the people was punished by a plague, Nu 25.1-9; As a general threat, Lev 18.25; for idolatry, Lev 26.14ff; as part of a general exhortation, Deut 8.19f; 11.1ff; 28ff.

7. Major sections of each of the prophetic books threatened the destruction because of Israel's sins or mourn for the Temple as does the *Book of Lamentations*. The Talmud frequently blamed the destruction on the sins of the people; see Kaufman Kohler, *Jewish Theology* (New York: 1927), pp. 342 ff.; in recent times various groups of Hassidim, including R. Teitelbaum, have seen the Holocaust as punishment for the sins of the people of Israel.

8. Ex 21.13; Nu 35.25-34; Josh 20.7, 8.

9. Gen 4.11-14; also in later legislation in Ex 21.14; Nu 35.20, 21; Deut 19.11; II Sam 14.7; II Sam 21.5-9.

10. Lev 19.18; Deut 24.16.

11. Lev 24.14 ff; I Kings 21.13; Josh 7.25.

12. Sabbath violation, Ex 31.14-15; 35.2; incitement to apostasy, Deut 13.2-12; presenting a child to Moloch, Lev 20.2-3; sacrifice to another deity, Deut 17.2-7; sorcery, Ex 22.17; cursing parents, Ex 20.9; adultery, Ex 20.10; homosexuality, Lev 20.13; incest, Ex 20. 11 ff; bestiality, Ex 20.15; rape of a betrothed girl, Deut 22.25; adultery , Gen 38.24; Lev 20.10; Deut 22.22; kidnapping, Ex 21.16; cursing the king, 1 K 21.10-16; 2 K 9.26; striking or cursing parents, Ex 21.15 and 17; not guarding a known goring ox, Ex 21.28 ff; Lev 20.9; false witness in a capital case, Deut 19.19; disregard of the court, Deut 17.8-13.

13. Ex 21.20, 16; Deut 8.5; 21.22-23; 25.2; Prov 19.18; 23.13; 29.17. In the Bible whipping was used as punishment when no other penalty was specifically mentioned, Deut 25.1, 2; 40 lashes was the maximum amount. Later exegesis disagreed about the limitations of this type of punishment, Mak 2b; Ibn Ezra to Deut 25.1, 2, etc.

14. Deut 13.13-18.

15. Nu 5.11-3; Prov 6.32-35 though some scholars like M. Greenberg in "Some Postulates of Biblical Criminal Law," *Yehezkel Kaufmann Jubilee Volume*, pp. 15 ff., felt that execution was mandatory.

16. Deut 22.13ff and 28.

17. Ex 21.24-25; 24.19; later Jewish law clearly indicated that monetary compensation was to be provided rather than literal retribution and the Biblical wording itself may already indicate that this was the path taken (B. Jacob, *Auge um Auge, Eine Untersuchung zum alten und Neuen Testament*, Berlin, 1929).
18. Ex 21.26, 27.
19. Deut 25.11, 12.
20. Deut 22.18; 25.1-3.
21. Prov 6.30f; Ex 21.37.
22. Ex 22.8.
23. Lev 5.24.
24. Lev 25; Deut 15.
25. Lev 24.12; Nu 15.34; 1 Kings 22.27; 2 Chron 16.10; Jer 37.15, 38.4-14; Ezra 7.25.
26. Ezra 7.26, 10.8.
27. Lev 19.15; 34-36; Deut 16.18ff; 24.17.
28. Much material scattered throughout the Talmud dealt with the Temple rituals. The initial discussions (Deut 17.14- 20; Joshua 1.18; 1 Samuel 1; 1 Kings 21) were expanded and detailed (San 5a; 49a; 52a, etc.).
29. Summaries of this material appear in H.L. Strack and G. Stemberger, *Introduction to the Talmud and Midrash* (Minneapolis: 1992) ; Z. H. Chajes, *The Student's Guide through the Talmud* (New York: 1960); H. Albeck, *Mavo Lamishnah* (Jerusalem: 1959); M. Elon, *Hamishpat Ha-Ivri* (Jerusalem: 1973).
30. San 10a and Rashi.
31. Mak 3.10f; San 10aff.
32. Mak 22 b.
33. Tem 3a. In those instances when two punishments were prescribed for the same crime, whipping gave way to monetary fines and reparation (Mak 1.2, 4b; Ket 32a, etc.).
34. J Suk. 55b; Yev 90b; Kid 81a.
35. Ket 86a.
36. MK 16a; Git 36b; Yev 89b; for repeat offenders (Baba Kama 96b)
37. Git 40b; 59a. The court retroactively seized the ring with which an abducted girl had been formally married and so invalidated her marriage (Yev 90b, 110a). There were similar uses of this power with wills (J Kid 159d; Ket 39a).
38. Git 36a ff
39. Yeb. 118 b; Git 44 a; B.K. 91 a; M.K. 16 a; fixed fines M. B.K. 8.6; M. Ket. 3.7; on the power of the courts see Asher b. Yehiel, *Responsa* 101.1; *Shulhan Arukh, Hoshen Mishpat*, 1.5.
40. M. San. 8.1ff.
41. San 52 a.
42. San 45a, 52 a.
43. M San 6.4; 45a. This may have followed the precedent of 2 Chr 25.12 or been done in imitation of Greek custom.
44. M San 7.2; 52a; we have no record of this form of execution being used, but we do learn of a priest's daughter burned for adultery and of this practice condemned when used by Hama ben Tobia (San 52a).
45. San 52a.
46. San 52b; 84b; 89a.
47. M San 6.1 ff.
48. M San 6.4, though there was some discussion about applying this to women.

49. San 43 a; Matt 27.34; Mark 15.23.
50. San 82 b; Ker 5 a.
51. Makkot 7a.
52. Pes 91a; Yoma 11a; J Pes 36a; Moed Katan 81c.
53. Moed Katan 16a.
54. 81 b-82 a.
55. J. Newman, *Semikhah* (Manchester, England: 1950), cited a number of opinions. It was the common consensus that ordination ceased after R. Hillel Hanasi (320-370), while H. J. Bornstein claimed that it continued until the time of Maimonides (1135-1205). Newman, himself, felt that it ended with David b. Azaria in 1062.
56. M. Ket 3.7; B K 8.6, though larger fines could be imposed by the court (Baba Kama 96 b).
57. J. Pes 30d.
58. M. Jung, *The Jewish Law of Theft* (New York: 1929); M. Elon, *Hamishpat Ha-ivri* (Jerusalem: 1973).
59. Ezra 10.8. Earlier it had referred to consecration to God (Lev 27.28; Nu 18.14, etc.), in conquest (Nu 21.2,3) as punishment (Ex 22.19; Deut 13.16), or as part of a vow (Jud 11.30).
60. Nu 12.14, though that punishment was limited to seven days.
61. Against scholars for unwillingness to comply with the majority decision (BM 59b); for various lay offenses (Kid 72a, Shab 130a, Pes 53a).
62. Moed Katan 16 a.
63. Mod Katan 15 a b; B M 59b, etc.
64. Ber 19a; they were later listed by Maimonides (*Yad, Hil. Talmud Torah* 6 and in the *Shulhan Arukh, Yoreh Deah* 334. The offenses are not related in any way.
65. M..San 3.1; San 5a; R.H. 25b. The death penalty could only be exercised by a court of 23 during the time when the court of 71 sat in the Chamber of Hewn Stone, which ceased before 70 C.E.
66. Asher ben Yehiel klal 101.1; Judah b. Asher, *Responsa (Zikhron Yehudah,* Jerusalem 1967) # 79 The courts were no longer a *bet din,* but the elders of the city. The justification was necessity, i.e. the problems of the hour, the need to create order out of chaos, the prevention of the wicked reigning supreme, the protection of the community, (Asher ben Yehiel, *Klal* 17.1, 6; Solomon b. Aderet, *Responsa,* 4.185; 5.238; and others. In addition there was the preventive measure of keeping Jewish affairs in the hands of the Jewish minority and out of the general courts, which would lead to the end of Jewish semi-autonomy, (Asher ben Yehiel, *Klal* 17.8) or to courts in which justice could not be guaranteed (*Yam shel Shelomo, Perek* 8. 7 quoting a Sephardic responsum). There was a special need to act against informers, so this was possible even on Yom Kippur which fell on shabbat (Asher ben Yehiel *Responsa* 107.6; Adret, *Responsa,* 1.80).

All of these common sense arguments were used and a new judiciary was created. It based itself on the older legal system and its penalties even though at times clearly recognizing that the justification was precarious.

As the fundamental nature of the judiciary had changed other changes followed with equally little justification from the past. As we look at the earlier courts and their medieval successors we will note many distinctions. The laws of evidence have been greatly relaxed and punishments changed. It was no longer necessary to have two absolutely certain witnesses, something already true for certain matters in Talmudic times. Often a single witness sufficed or women were permitted to testify. Centuries later there was still astonishment at minor and major changes. Isaac b. Sheshet (1326 Valencia -1408 Algiers) was astonished that witnesses were sworn, contrary to rabbinic law (Kid 43b—Tosfos), which changed the nature of of testimony. Furthermore women, specifically excluded (Kid 73b) from being witnesses were regularly included; a decision of Rabenu Tam, *Responsa* 179, Meir of Rothenburg, *Responsa*, 4.185. Evidence which in earlier times would have been considered hearsay was also admitted depending on the nature of the crime and the general circumstances (*Yam shel Shelomo* 8.7).

67. *Shaarei Zedek*, 4.7.38; *Or Zarua* 1.112; Assaf cited a large number of authorities who decreed the death penalty, especially in Spain; they included Moses Maimonides; Joseph Ibn Migash, Solomon b. Adret. S. Simcha Assaf, *Op. Cit.*, pp. 19 ff.

68. S. Assaf, *Otzar Hageonim*, pp. 21ff.

69. Ibid., pp. 25ff.

70. Ibid., p. 27.

71. Ibid., pp. 92, 121, 155, 313

72. Ibi.d., pp. 24, 59, 89, 93.

73. *Yad Hil. San* 17ff.

74. Whipping Monday, Thursday and the following Monday for a false oath, Jacob Judah Weil, *Responsa* # 123; R. Isaac of Narbonne ordered a daily whipping, morning and evening, for a year in addition to fasting as penitence for manslaughter while under the influence of alcohol, Abraham b. Isaac of Narbonne, *Responsa* # 41.

75. S. Assaf, *Otzar Hageonim,*. pp. 23ff.

76. *Yad Hil. San.* 19 and numerous responsa.

77. S. Assaf, *Op. Cit.*, 95, 127, 133, 137, 141; fines were also imposed for not accepting the authority of the rabbis. Asher, *Responsa* 21.8 or using a non-Jewish court to settle a dispute *Mordecai B. K.* 195.

78. *Yam shel Shelomo B.K.* 8.49; *Shulhan Arukh, Yoreh Deah* 256.1; Asher ben Yehiel, *Responsa* 13.4; 21.8.

79. *Shulhan Arukh, Yoreh Deah* 334; the hardship which this imposed on the family was opposed by some rabbis: Asher b. Yehiel, *Responsa* 43.9; Isaac b. Sheshet, *Responsa* 173; Solomon Adret, *Responsa* 5.238; *Yam shel Shelomo B.K.* 10.13.

80. A system of penance was discussed by Eliezer b. Judah of Worms, *Rokeah* 2; a selection of authorities from various centuries, who prescribed penance in their responsa, include Abraham b. Isaac of Narbonne, *Responsa* # 41; Jacob b. Judah Weil, *Responsa* # 123; Moses Isserles, Responsa # 37; Moses Sofer, *Responsa Hatam Sofer, Orah Hayyim* # 166; a long list of such responsa may be found in Isaac Lampronti, *Pahad Yitzhok*, Vol. 10, pp. 175ff.

81. Radbaz, *Responsa*, # 187; Bacharach, *Responsa* # 141; Morpurgo, *Responsa, Yoreh Deah* # 48.

❖   ❖   ❖

Chapter 5

CAPITAL PUNISHMENT

Rabbi Richard A. Block

The question is as old as human history and as fresh as today's headlines: May those who violate society's most fundamental norms be put to death? Timothy McVeigh is the convict *du jour* and for the purpose of assaying an answer to that question, his case is as good as any and perhaps better than most. After all, if McVeigh's crime does not warrant the death penalty, what does? But let us recall, as we begin, that McVeigh's execution, if it occurs, may be ten or more years away and the US death row population presently exceeds 3,200 persons, 41 percent of them black. Seventy-nine people were executed in the United States in 1996 and each year approximately 300 more are sentenced to death.[1] By the time America's official killing machine spews forth Timothy McVeigh's corpse, more than a thousand men and women are likely to precede him and several thousand more will be waiting in line.

If my position is not already evident, let me state it explicitly: I oppose capital punishment on Jewish and social grounds that I will outline later, but I did not arrive at this position easily nor do

---

I regard it as inevitable. If I have contributed anything to the discussion of capital punishment and Jewish tradition within the Reform Movement, it has been to challenge the conventional wisdom and demonstrate that in Jewish tradition as a whole, not just the Torah, support for the death penalty is an authentic, Jewishly tenable position. Indeed, it is arguably the normative one.

The official position of the Reform Movement opposing capital punishment has been stated numerous times, including a 1959 UAHC General Assembly resolution and CCAR resolutions in 1958, 1960 and 1979. The latter states its opposition to all forms of capital punishment ... under all circumstances" and expresses the "[un]shaken ... conviction" that "[b]oth in concept and practice, Jewish tradition found capital punishment repugnant, despite Biblical sanctions for it."[2] As I hope to demonstrate, notwithstanding my own position, this statement is plainly wrong.

The Torah prescribes capital punishment for a wide variety of offenses, from murder and kidnapping to adultery, Shabbat violation, and abuse of parents. Its enactments in this regard are so extensive and well known as not to require citation. Modern rabbinic exhortations against capital punishment, while acknowledging the Torah's position, generally rely upon a famous mishnah in Tractate *Makkot*: "A Sanhedrin that puts one man to death in a week [of years] is called 'destructive.' R. Eleazer b. Azariah says: Or one in even seventy years. R. Tarphon and R. Akiba say: Had we been in the Sanhedrin none would ever have been put to death."[3]

Note well, however, that while Rabbis Tarphon and Akiba may be said to oppose capital punishment, Rabbi Eleazar does not rule it out entirely. Moreover, the anonymous mishnah, which presents the authoritative position, holds that the death penalty should be imposed infrequently, not never. Since this is a view that even thoughtful supporters of capital punishment may share, reliance on this text as the mainstay of the argument for abolition is misplaced.

A more serious flaw is the common failure to cite the remainder of the mishnah, in which we learn, "Rabban Simeon b. Gamaliel says, 'They [who would not impose the death penalty] would multiply shedders of blood in Israel.' " Our colleague, Julius Kravetz z'l, described the "edited" citation of *Makkot* 1:10 as a "scandalous example of ... deliberately induced tunnel vision,"[4] and observed, "[T]hose who have been moved by what they regarded as nobler and more humane sentiments ... have not been inhibited by the scruples of academic fastidiousness in their ... exploitation of the tradition.[5]

Far from proving the case against capital punishment, the text demonstrates that Jewish post-biblical tradition contains a range of views, which are mirrored in today's policy debates. It reflects a fundamental tension between a reverence for human life so profound that it embraces even the most despicable criminal and society's right to take all measures necessary to protect its citizens and insure its own survival.

If additional evidence be needed that the Jewish post-biblical tradition does not find capital punishment conceptually "repugnant" it is plentiful. Tractate Sanhedrin, in significant part, is a virtual executioner's manual.[6] It sets out and describes, *ad nauseum*, the four methods of execution considered legal in Jewish capital cases: stoning, burning, decapitation and strangulation.[7] For Maimonides, each of these is a distinct *mitzvah*; hence they collectively constitute four of the 613 commandments.[8] Of the four, strangulation was preferred by the rabbis because it was the one that did least injury to the body. The person would be sunk to the knees in mud and then strangled with a hard cloth wrapped in a soft one which was twisted around his neck and pulled in opposite directions until he suffocated.[9]

Talmudic sources explicitly affirm that the needs of society can justify the death penalty[10] even when the Torah does not classify the crime as a capital offense, so long as the punishment is required "to safeguard" the Torah.[11] Death is held to be the just and appropriate punishment for numerous crimes and to effectuate the principle of *midah keneged midah* when a life has been taken.[12] We also find talmudic support for the notion that capital punishment was preventative.[13] Since capital punishment was held to expiate the crime, it was also said to be in the interest of both society and the defendant.[14] Ultimately, capital punishment was understood to represent just retribution. As the Mishnah states, "And lest you say, 'Why should we be guilty of the blood of this man?' was it not already said, 'When the wicked perish there is rejoicing.'"[15] We may or may not share these views, but they clearly support the Torah's jurisprudence and demonstrate that, as De Sola Pool concluded, "It [is] beyond doubt that the Rabbis approved of the theory of capital punishment."[16]

May we yet say that the CCAR resolution was half right, that Jewish tradition rejects capital punishment in practice? Or, as

Gerald Blidstein concluded, that "Jewish law abolished capital punishment in fact not by denying its conceptual moral validity but rather by allowing it *only* this conceptual validity?" I had this view in mind earlier when I referred to the "conventional wisdom." This claim builds on a host of talmudic rules of evidence and criminal procedure, chief among them *hatra'ah*, the requirement that a person be warned, just prior to the crime and in the presence of two witnesses, that he is liable to be executed should he commit the act,[17] which warning must be acknowledged immediately and unequivocally.[18] Some authorities went so far as to insist that the warning include the manner of execution.[19] At trial, the witnesses were to be examined closely[20] and separately.[21] Inconsistencies in their testimony, even about matters immaterial to the crime itself, barred the imposition of the death penalty.[22]

Do these rules prove that the rabbis supported capital punishment in theory, but abolished it in practice? I believe that they do not, for several reasons. Firstly, their effect is not to eliminate capital punishment, but to restrict it to cases where there is clear, convincing, and uncontradicted evidence of guilt, criminal intent, and premeditation. Moreover, the rules were not enforced inflexibly. Thus, for example, scholars could be executed without *hatra'ah*. Since "warning is only a means of deciding whether one has committed the crime willfully or not,"[23] it was unnecessary when willfulness could be inferred from a defendant's presumed knowledge of the law. Jewish tradition also allows *batei din* to impose extraordinary punishment and disregard normal evidentiary and procedural rules as an emergency measure.[24]

Secondly, Jewish courts lost their authority to impose capital punishment after the destruction of the Temple in 70 C.E., [25] and, even presuming that these restrictions predated that event, there is scant evidence that they were ever employed in a functioning Jewish criminal justice system. In addition, as we shall see, when Jews regained that authority in later times and other places, they imposed capital punishment notwithstanding these seemingly insurmountable barriers. Thus, like the talmudic descriptions of execution methodology, the Talmud's stringent procedural and evidentiary rules are to be regarded as largely theoretical, not as evidence of actual practice.

Thirdly, recognizing the detrimental effect on justice and social welfare that might occur if imposing capital punishment became impossible, Jewish tradition provides an extra-judicial avenue to rectify the matter. Thus, wholly apart from the Jewish court system, tradition confers on the monarch the authority to administer what Maimonides calls *din ha-malkhut,* i.e., "the sovereign's justice."[26] Unlike a *bet din,* a Jewish monarch is empowered to act for the benefit of society by executing criminals even when the crime is not a capital offense under biblical law.[27] In addition, the monarch is not bound by the strict laws of evidence to which the Jewish court is subject. Thus, for example, the monarch can impose the death penalty on the basis of one witness or a confession.[28] Whether circumstantial evidence is a sufficient basis for capital punishment as an exercise of sovereign justice is not clear, [29] but even without clear proof or warning, "the king has authority to execute [a criminal] and to perfect the world in accordance with what the hour requires."[30] As Rabbi David Bleich observes, "Jewish law provides ... in effect ... two separate systems of justice and two parallel judiciaries."[31]

Ultimately, the best evidence of Jewish legal practice is derived not from legislation, but from history. The Mishnah indicates that persons charged with capital offenses were sometimes executed, even if *hatra'ah* had not occurred or there were evidentiary problems, so long as the court was certain of guilt.[32] The Talmud also informs us that after Jewish courts lost the authority to impose capital punishments, murderers were turned over to civil authorities for execution,[33] a practice that continued into the Middle Ages.[34]

Finally, capital punishment was carried out by Jewish authorities, both before and after 70 C.D.E., when it was possible, whether strictly in accordance with the law or not.[35] To cite but a few examples, the Talmud recounts a man being stoned to death "in the Greek period" for riding a horse on Shabbat.[36] In another instance, a woman and a young man whom she had raised from infancy were brought to a *bet din* and stoned to death for incest.[37] The case is all the more noteworthy for the fact that there was no proof that he was her son, the sentence being imposed after presuming that fact because "he clinged to her."[38] Simeon ben Shetah, who declined to impose the death penalty in one case involving overwhelming circumstantial evidence,[39] is said, nonetheless, to have hanged eighty women in Ashkelon,[40] and in 240 C.E., Origen declares in a letter that the Jewish patriarch in Palestine exercised the power to impose and carry out capital punishment.[41]

In the post-talmudic era, too, Jewish courts were sometimes empowered to impose the death penalty. (Asher ben Jehiel, also known as Rosh) attests to the practice in 14th century Spain,[42] and himself imposed it on an informer.[43] Maimonides declares that killing informers or handing them over to non-Jews to be killed was a regular occurrence "in the cities of the West."[44] Jews were also granted the power to impose capital punishment in North Africa[45] and 17th century Lithuania.[46]

One scholar summarized as follows, "From all of these decisions and incidents we have seen that in every period the important rabbinic authorities of Israel, men of renown, imposed capital punishment on Jewish criminals if they considered the matter imperative to deter wrongdoers."[47] Another, Justice Haim H. Cohn of the Supreme Court of Israel, put it this way,

> Though in strict law the competence to inflict capital punishment ceased with the destruction of the Temple, Jewish courts continued, whenever they had the power ... to pass and execute death sentences ... not even necessarily for capital offenses as defined in the law, but also for offenses considered in the circumstances prevailing at the time, as particularly dangerous or obnoxious ... In order not to give the appearance of exercising sanhedrical jurisdiction, they would ... normally refrain from using any of the four legal modes of execution; but isolated instances are found of stoning, slaying and strangling, along with such newly devised or imitated modes of execution as starvation in a subterranean pit, drowning, bleeding or delivery into the hands of official executioners. In most cases, however the manner in which the death sentences were to be executed was probably left to the persons who were authorized or assigned by the court to carry them out.[48]

Clearly, just as the rabbis approved of capital punishment in theory, they utilized it in practice, though seemingly rarely and with reluctance. While the Talmud indeed contains two antithetical bodies of material on capital punishment, it is a mistake to view one as theoretical and the other as practical. Rather, they are both largely theoretical and reflect the classic tension between *midat hadin* and *midat harakhamim*. The Talmud's gory and detailed accounts of execution methods amount to a rabbinic relief map of "the attribute of justice." Strict justice demands the death of the sinner for serious crimes against people and God. Talmudic restrictions on capital punishment constitute a rabbinic atlas of "the attribute of mercy." Mercy pleads for a concession to human weakness and an opportunity to do *teshuvah*.

All of this, however, has little if any bearing on the McVeigh case, from the standpoint of Jewish tradition. Like the vast majority of American criminal defendants, *barukh haShem*, McVeigh is a non-Jewish defendant in a gentile court. What does Jewish tradition teach about such a situation?

In this regard, the seven commandments of *b'nai Noach* come into play. The Noahide code prohibits murder, theft and sexual immorality and requires that established violators of the code may be, or in the view of some, must be punished by imposing the death penalty.[49] Jewish law provides that in gentile courts the testimony of a single eyewitness suffices for conviction and execution, but the admissibility of confessions is a matter of dispute.[50] It is unclear whether capital punishment may be imposed on the basis of circumstantial evidence.[51] Rabbi David Bleich cites a statement by Rambam in *Guide the Perplexed*[52] that a gentile sovereign may do so and reasons as follows: Since gentile courts are empowered to enforce the provisions of the Noahide code and possess delegated authority to impose "the sovereign's justice," it can be strongly argued that such courts *may* impose capital punishment on the basis of circumstantial evidence, as in the case of Timothy McVeigh.

Where does this leave the committed Jew who seeks to ground his or her position on capital punishment in Jewish tradition? In the final analysis, Jewish tradition is ambivalent about capital punishment and the claim that there is only one coherent, Jewish authentic position on the subject strikes me as intellectually dishonest and morally flawed. As I observed in 1983, in an article in The Journal of Reform Judaism:[53] "Such a position can emerge [only] from a personal confrontation with Jewish tradition, as one draws upon the part of the tradition that resonates most intense within oneself."

For me, the most resonant aspect of the tradition is its reluctance to take a human life, even a life that "deserves" to be taken, its reluctance to become a killer in response to a killing. Society certainly has the right—ought indeed, it has the obligation—to protect itself by punishing criminals, but it ought not kill criminals on the unproved and unprovable supposition that capital punishment saves lives by deterring crime.

Capital punishment may be just, but it cannot be administered in a just, fair and uniform manner. Our legal system is the finest humanity has ever known, but it is far from perfect. Its chief fuel is money, and its chief flaw is that only the affluent defendant can be sure of receiving an adequate defense. The history of capital punishment in western civilization in general, and in this country in particular, demonstrates that the poor, members of racial and ethnic minorities, and the physically ugly are disproportionately likely to be executed for capital crimes. As a well-known American attorney once put it, "I've never seen a rich man go to the chair."

Moreover, cases in which innocent people have been wrongly convicted of capital crimes are disturbingly common. Even when there is eyewitness identification or a confession, the identification sometimes turns out to have been incorrect or the confession is revealed to have been coerced or falsified. Once a person has been executed, the injustice cannot be undone. The risk of executing innocent people cannot be eliminated so long as capital punishment is practiced. The essence of the problem is captured well in the title of a 1974 book by the eminent constitutional scholar, Charles L. Black: *Capital Punishment: The Inevitability of Caprice and Mistake.*[54]

In addition, society should not resort to capital punishment if there are less drastic means of achieving the public policy goals of criminal law. One means of deterring crime and protecting innocent people would be to devote adequate resources to law enforcement. We do not know whether capital punishment deters crime, but we do know that crime decreases as the certainty of punishment increases, whatever the punishment may be. A second means of deterring crime and protecting the innocent would be to impose a genuine life sentence. A person who commits a truly heinous crime can be locked up, safely away from society, for life, without possibility of parole. Society does not need to kill killers in order to protect itself.

These reasons for opposing capital punishment are not uniquely Jewish, but they emerge from a tradition that values both justice and mercy and strives to accommodate both demands. They emerge from a tradition keenly aware that human life could not exist in a world of strict justice, but that human society could not exist in a world of pure mercy. They emerge from a tradition that teaches us that God prays. What is God's prayer? "May My attribute of mercy overcome My attribute of anger."[55] Even God's prayer may not always be answered, but its guiding direction is clear.

Notes

1. *Time* 149, 24 (June 19, 1997): 34-35.
2. *CCAR Yearbook* 89: 105.
3. M.Mak. 1:10.
4. Julius Kravetz, "Some Cautionary Remarks," *CCAR Journal* 15, 1 (January, 1968): 75; see Passamanek, *supra*, p. 16.
5. Ibid.
6. See, e.g., San. 49b, *et seq.*
7. M. San. 7:1.
8. J. David Bleich, *Contemporary Halachic Problems* II, p. 350.
9. M.San. 7:3.
10. M.San. 8:5: San. 46a: Yeb. 90b.
11. San. 46a; Yeb. 90b.
12. See, e.g., M.Sota 1:7 and M.San. 4:5.
13. As in the instance of the defiant and rebellious son, M.San. 8:5; San. 72a; Sifre Deut. xxi, 18-21. This example is to be regarded as theoretical, since the rabbis also insisted that there never was nor would there ever be a son who warranted this punishment. Nonetheless, if one speaks of the rabbis' conceptual understanding of capital punishment, the text has direct bearing.
14. M.San. 9:5 and Tos.San. 9:5. The latter recounts a case of a person taken out for stoning for an unspecified offense and indicates that "those executed by a *bet din* have a share of the world to come because they are confessed of all their sins."
15. M.San. 4:5, quoting Prov. 11:10.
16. D. De Sola Pool, *Capital Punishment Among the Jews* (New York, 1916), p. 20.
17. San. 8b, 9b, *inter alia*.
18. San. 40b.
19. San 8b,Mak.16a.
20. San. 32b.
21. San. 29a.
22. San. 40b.
23. San. 8b.
24. Bleich, p. 353, note 12; Rambam, *Hilkhot Rotzeah* 2:4, *Hilkhot Mamrim* 2:4.
25. San. 37b; Sota 8b; Ket. 30a. See also, NT, John 18:31. Josephus, *The Jewish Wars* 6, ii, 4 and Bleich, p. 343.
26. Rambam, *Hilkhot Rotzeah* 2:4 and *Hilkhot Sanhedrin* 8:6. See also, Bleich, pp. 350-56.
27. Bleich, p. 351. notes 10 and 11.
28. Rambam, *Hilkhot Sanhedrin* 18:6.
29. Bleich, p. 355. and note 16.
30. Rambam, *Hilkhot Melakhim 3:10, Hilkhot Rotzeah 2:4.*
31. Bleich, p. 350. In effect, the Jewish sovereign may be said to enforce the Noahide code against his or her subjects when the restrictions of the Sinaitic code are too stringent. See the discussion of the Noahide code at p.7, *infra.*
32. San. 9:5 and rabbinic commentaries, including Rashi and Bertinoro. See also Kravetz, note 3, page 81.

33. San. 37b; Sota 8b: Ket. 30a. The texts indicate that such defendants were turned over for decapitation, the form of execution prescribed for murder. San.9: 1; Mechilta to Exodus 21:12.
34. De Sola Pool, *supra*, note 10, pp. 47-50; Blidstein, *supra*, note 12, pp.170-71: Haim H. Cohn, "Capital Punishment," *Encyclopedia Judaica* 5:144 (Jerusalem, 1972).
35. San. 6:4, 7:2; Tos.San. 9:5, 9:11; San. 46a, 52b; Git. 57a; Kid. 80a; Ber.58a.
36. San. 46a; J. Chag. 2:14, 78a.
37. Kid. 80a.
38. Ibid.
39. San. 37b.
40. M.San. 6:4.
41. Ep.ad.African. Par.14. Juster, I.C.,p. 151, note 2. Cited by De Sola Pool, *supra* 41-42.
42. *Teshuvot ha-Rosh,* k'lal 17, no. 8.
43. *Teshuvot ha-Rosh,* k'lal 16, no. 1.
44. *Yad. Hikhot Hobel u'Mazik* 8:2.
45. De Sola Pool, supra pp. 48-50.
46. "Lithuania," *The Jewish Encyclopedia,* vol. 8 (New York, 1904), p. 129.
47. Jacob M. Ginsberg, *Mishpatim LeYisrael* (Jerusalem, 1956), p. 26.
48. Haim H. Cohn. "Capital Purnshment," *Encyclopedia Judaica,* vol. 5 (Jerusalem, 1972), p. 144.
49. Rambam holds that capital punishment is mandatory. Others understand the gentile courts to have discretionary authority in this regard. See Bleich, pp. 344-347.
50. Ibid.
51. Ibid.
52. Book 3, chapter 40; Bleich, pp. 365-66.
53. "Death, Thou Shalt Die: Reform Judaism and Capital Punishment," *Journal of Reform Judaism,* Spring (1983): 1-10.
54. Norton, 1974.
55. Ber. 7a.

Chapter 6

❖   ❖   ❖

CONFRONTATION OF HALAKHAH
AND RELIGIOUS VIOLENCE

Moshe Zemer

When I was a young graduate student at the Hebrew University in Jerusalem, the only orthodox religious disturbance that I encountered were occasional shouts of "Shabbas!" when a vehicle would pass infrequently through a religious neighborhood on Shabbat. This was the extent of religious violence that I experienced in Israel during my student days. As the years went by, these occasional shouts turned into verbal violence, eventually leading to violent demonstrations, with stone throwing and attacks on individuals suspected of having violated the Sabbath or other commandments of the Torah.

Most distressing is the fact that precisely those who claim to be the guardian of the fortress of halakhah are those who desecrate the Torah, both its letter and its spirit, through their violent demonstrations. We should make plain that not only do their actions violate the laws of the state and undermine the foundations of democracy, they also contravene halakhah, in whose name they are ostensibly acting.

Notes for this section begin on page 87.

Desecrating the Shabbat in Order to Sanctify it

Ultra-Orthodox demonstrations in Jerusalem fit into a larger picture of violence by members of that community. Although such violent demonstrations are evidently in pursuit of political and material gains, leaders of the Ultra-Orthodox community always adduce the halakhic concepts of preserving the Sabbath and observing the Torah to explain them.

Does halakhah really sanction such violent demonstrations? To answer this question we must clarify whether demonstrations by the ultra-Orthodox themselves constitute desecration of the Sabbath. If they do, we must determine whether it is permitted to desecrate the Sabbath in order to preserve its sanctity and whether these demonstrations expand the circle of Sabbath observance among non-Orthodox Jews.

Unfortunately, there is no escaping the conclusion that the ultra-Orthodox campaign to defend the Sabbath in Jerusalem and elsewhere in Israel involves public desecration of the Sabbath. The battle to increase Sabbath observance has actually increased Sabbath desecration. Violence has become an inseparable part of the Sabbath demonstrations and a normal method of applying massive pressure to achieve the objectives of the ultra-Orthodox leadership with regard to many other issues. On weekdays, too, there have been violent disturbances over archaeological excavations or "pornographic" pictures on bus shelters, assaults on peaceful citizens who were minding their own business, and even the desecration of graves.

A survey of the media indicates how deeply rooted in these circles is the use of violence as a means of persuasion. Bottles and rocks have been hurled at policemen in downtown Jerusalem from time to time; the "sport" of stoning traffic on the suburban Ramot road went on for four full years. Nor has this Sabbath violence been limited to the capital. On the mall in Haifa, too, a large group of ultra-Orthodox ruffians beat up three journalists who had come to observe a mass prayer rally.

In the spring of 1984, the chief rabbi of Petah Tikvah, speaking at the end of a mass rally on behalf of Sabbath observance, called for action against the public desecration of the Sabbath by a local coffee house. The result, according to media reports, was that ultra-Orthodox demonstrators, led by their rabbi, "ripped off the metal door and forced their way inside. Fistfights quickly developed and blows were exchanged .... During the disturbances, windows were broken, tables overturned, and bottles smashed."[1]

In addition to contravening the laws of the state, these and similar acts also involved forbidden labor on the Sabbath. According to halakhah, if there were two witnesses present who warned that they were about to desecrate the Sabbath, the perpetrators were liable to the death penalty by stoning (Maimonides, *Laws of the Sabbath* 1:2).

The years of Sabbath riots on the Ramot road in suburban Jerusalem gave rise to sad thoughts concerning our ability to live as equal citizens in a free Jewish state, despite our differences. In any case, the Chief Rabbinate and official religious establishment stood aside and generally maintained perfect silence on this matter. Do they realize that "silence is tacit acknowledgment" (BT Yevamot 87b)?

Particularly worrisome is the attitude of one of the leaders of Neturei Karta, Rabbi Moshe Hirsch, as reported on Israel Radio in September 1979. Rabbi Hirsch offered halakhic arguments that ostensibly justify the use of force to preserve the nature of the Sabbath as he understands it. He also offered a "halakhic solution" to the crisis. Let us investigate the halakhic basis of this rabbi's arguments.

Zealots Attack Him

Rabbi Hirsch found support for the violence on the Ramot road in a well-known Mishnah: "If a man stole a sacred vessel or cursed by means of witchcraft or had sexual relations with a [gentile] woman—zealots may attack him" (Mishnah Sanhedrin 9:6). The Sages held that even though the Torah does not stipulate the death penalty for those guilty of such misdeeds, those who are zealous for the Lord have permission to assault and kill them.

Throwing stones at passing cars on the Ramot road is quite remote from the cases mentioned in the Talmud and by later codifiers. What is more, Rabbi Hirsch seems to have forgotten or purposely suppressed an important element in the license granted to zealots. According to the Gemara, this justifiable zealousness must be a spontaneous and unplanned act: "Rabbi Hisda said: If a person comes to ask [whether he may assault someone who has profaned the sacred] we do not instruct him to do so" (BT Sanhedrin 82a).

Therefore, there is no permission to harm or attack a Sabbath-desecrator if the zealousness is not a spontaneous emotional outburst. The carefully planned activity organized in the ultra-Orthodox neighborhoods, such as Me'ah She'arim, far from the Ramot road, were not spontaneous by any standard and could hardly satisfy the halakhic criterion that licenses those zealous for the Lord to give vent to their pent-up feelings.

Rabbi Hirsch, other ultra-Orthodox leaders, and their followers who hurled stones and bottles at vehicles clearly believe that they may desecrate the Sabbath in order to keep others from desecrating it. No one has ever stated the source of this permission, probably for the simple reason that it is not to be found anywhere in the codified halakhah. Not only are these actions by the ultra-Orthodox crimes against the laws of the state, they are also severe violations of the Sabbath.

It is permitted to desecrate the Sabbath for only one reason—to save lives; that is, saving human life (*pikkuah nefesh*) takes precedence over observance of the Sabbath. The underlying principle is based on the Biblical verse: "And the Children of Israel shall keep the Shabbat" (Exodus 31:16) which is interpreted by the Talmud to mean "The Torah tells us: desecrate one Sabbath for his sake so that he may observe many Sabbaths" (BT Yoma 85b).

Desecrating the holy Sabbath to save a human life aims in fact at augmenting its holiness through the observance of the Sabbath and other precepts in the future. The desecration of the Sabbath by the ultra-Orthodox in Jerusalem does not and cannot increase the prospects of Sabbath observance in the future or augment its sanctity. In fact it has quite the opposite effect, because it leads to further radicalization of the nonreligious population as well.

Instead of educating nonreligious people and helping them experience the wonderful value of Sabbath observance, ultra-Orthodox zealousness and extremism repulse them and push them further away from Jewish tradition.

The periodical of the religious kibbutz movement (*Hakibbutz Hadati*) published the following evaluation of the results of the zealots' approach: "Seclusive ultra-Orthodoxy as the option of escape, weakness, and abandoning the majority of the people is … a prescription for failure. It is a fact that the vast majority of the *secular* and even *antireligious* adult population was a *product of the ultra- Orthodox path* but fell away from it in the recent generations of secularism."[2]

Two Who Laid Hold of a Tallit

Rabbi Hirsch and the ultra-Orthodox Council in Jerusalem offered a miracle solution to the quarrel over the Ramot road. The solution was based on seeing the road as falling into the category of the disputed mishnaic *tallit:* "If two people laid hold of a *tallit* and one says ... "it's all mine,' and the other says, "it's all mine'" (Mishnah Bava Metzia 1:1). In such a case, the Sages ruled, the *tallit* was to be torn in half and divided fifty-fifty. The Ultra-Orthodox rabbis wanted to apply this halakhic principle as follows: For two weeks the residents of Ramot would be allowed to travel on the new road that passes by the ultra-Orthodox neighborhood of Kiryat Sanz; for the next two weeks, they would travel by the old road, which passes by the Orthodox neighborhood of Sanhedrin. In this way they would split the experience of Sabbath desecration with a religious neighborhood that had so far remained aloof from the violence. If the road is the *tallit,* who were the two claimants holding on to it? The ultra-Orthodox from Kiryat Sanz, the residents of Ramot, or the religious residents of Sanhedrin? What sort of partition is being proposed? Is it not rather more like the solution proposed by King Solomon to the two harlots who asserted maternity of a single child—namely, that the child be cut in two? The implementation of such a division is so absurd that it was not given any serious consideration.

All of these attempted justifications are in reality only pseudo-halakhic arguments without any basis in Jewish law. This same sort of reasoning was used to justify vicious attacks on pathologists for performing autopsies and on archaeologists for desecrating grave sites.

Some would have us ignore the facts and blindly accept the ultra-Orthodox contention that the violence is an anomaly in their struggle, that their demonstrations are usually calm and orderly. Even if this were so, we must ask whether halakhah permits demonstrating and waging furious campaigns, as the ultra-Orthodox have repeatedly done on the Sabbath. Many of the actions associated with the demonstrations are themselves forbidden by halakhah. For example, one of the rabbinic dicta that might impinge on the Sabbath demonstrations is that one may not run or jump on the Sabbath. Maimonides phrased this as "you should not walk on the Sabbath as you do on weekdays." (*Laws of*

Sabbath 24:4; compare the ruling by Rabbi Moses Isserles that it is forbidden to take a step on the Shabbat of more than a cubit's length (56 centimeters or 22 inches) (*Shulhan Arukh O.H.* 301:1).

Even when they are not running, the way in which the ultra-Orthodox speak is a violation of the Sabbath. According to Maimonides, "you should not speak on the Sabbath in the fashion you speak on weekdays" (ibid.). According to the press, these demonstrations are regularly accompanied by shouts of "Shabbes! Shabbes!" and curses against the municipality, the police, and cinema-goers. Such loud and uncouth speech is utterly forbidden on the Sabbath.

In fact, and as a general rule, all disputes are forbidden on the Sabbath. According to the prominent twentieth-century decisor Rabbi Israel Meir Kagan of Radun, known as the Hafetz Hayyim (1838-1933), "the Zohar and the kabbalists warned strictly against any dispute on the Sabbath, Heaven forbid."[3] Yet the rabbis of the ultra-Orthodox community, who should have expert knowledge of the Sabbath halakhot, provoked a severe quarrel almost every Sabbath. By so doing, they violated the ruling of Rabbi Hayyim Joseph David Azulai (1724-1806): "On the Sabbath it is strictly forbidden to stir up quarrels or to get angry and it is twice as severe as when done on a weekday.[4]

These rabbinic prohibitions stand in utter contrast to the nature of protests in which demonstrators push against police barricades and chase nonreligious youth on the Sabbath. Such behavior is forbidden even during the week; how much the more so on the holy Sabbath! It is hard to understand why the chief rabbis and the Chief Rabbinate Council, an official state body, never issued a pronouncement calling on the observant to refrain from demonstrations that profane the Sabbath.

It is equally hard to understand how a pious Jew, who maintains that Torah is his profession, can fail to understand that he must distance himself from every form of Sabbath desecration. Apparently the ultra-Orthodox rabbis, eminent Torah scholars, do not teach their students that such is their obligation.

Have the ultra-Orthodox nevertheless found a halakhic precedent that gives them a license to desecrate the Sabbath or to prevent Sabbath desecration by others? If they have such permission, they should publish it for all to read. Both their silence and intensive halakhic research indicate, however, that there is no such ruling anywhere in the rabbinic literature.

It is an iron-clad rule that extremism on one side leads to radicalization on the other. We must take sorrowful note of an intensification of antireligious violence, such as the vandalizing of a synagogue in South Tel Aviv and the cutting off of the side curls of a boy in Jerusalem. These and similar incidents are a reaction to the protracted violence of the ultra-Orthodox. If the acts of religious coercion and violence continue, the extremely religious are liable to antagonize the younger generation, which has not yet rebelled against the Jewish religion.

Particularly astonishing and disappointing is the fact that the ultra-Orthodox approach utterly ignores the supreme precept to love one's fellow Jews, as stated by Maimonides: "Every man is commanded to love each and every Jew as himself, as it is stated, 'Love your neighbor as yourself'" (*Laws of Beliefs*, 6:3).

We sorely miss the perspective of Rabbi Abraham Isaac Kook, the first Ashkenazi chief rabbi of Eretz Israel, who discerned sparks of holiness in the secular Zionist enterprise and endeavored to draw all the non-observant toward the Jewish religion with "golden cords."[5] His approach was based on a profound faith in the value of each and every Jew as such, even if he or she does not observe the *mitzvot*. His words are important to the ultra-Orthodox in Me'ah She'arim and to all of us, whenever we are embroiled in potentially catastrophic quarrels like that on the Ramot road: "Even from the profane, the sacred may be revealed, and even from libertine freedom the cherished yoke." This approach, which finds something positive in every Jew and attempts to bring them closer, rather than repel them, is what we need if we are to survive the worsening crisis between the religious and nonreligious sectors in Israel.

Halakhic Apologia for Murder

We have seen the attempts to justify religious violence from sources of the halakhah, which indeed prohibits such acts. Since those earlier days of squabbles, stoning vehicles, and beating individuals in enraged political protests, we have witnessed an escalation to bloodshed. This problem has reached a point which is no longer concerned with minor political gains of closing a road or an archaeological site. Here there is an attempt to eliminate physically the enemy, whether it be a peaceful congregation of worshipers or the duly elected Head of State.

On Friday morning, February 25, 1994, Dr. Baruch Goldstein, a resident of the Jewish town of Kiryat Arba on the outskirts of Hebron, entered the Isaac Hall in the Tomb of the Patriarchs (known as the Ibrahimi Mosque), where the Muslim Ramadan service was taking place. Wearing his army reservist's uniform with its captain's bars, he was neither stopped nor suspected, even by the Arabs at prayer. Positioning himself behind the congregation, he raised his Galil assault rifle and emptied four magazines into the backs of the worshipers, killing twenty-nine and wounding perhaps twice as many before he was overpowered and killed by some of the Arabs.

Only at first sight was this appalling massacre the act of a single person. It is true that Baruch Goldstein carried out his murderous rampage alone, but he would not have committed twenty-nine murders without ideological and social backing. Goldstein, a physician who violated the Hippocratic Oath and shot down defenseless worshipers in a holy shrine, was nurtured by a warped and distorted faith that many shared with him.

We all think we know where this poison came from. Goldstein was a fervent supporter of the late Meir Kahane. He absorbed his mentor's racist doctrines, which pretend to be derived from halakhic sources, and put them into practice.

In Kahane's book, *Know Your Judaism (in Truth),* he could find the following rabbinic aphorisms: "Only non-Jews are cruel" (Maimonides, *Mishneh Torah,* Laws of Gifts to the Poor 10:2); "You [Israel] are called 'human'; but non-Jews are not called 'human'" (BT Bava Metzia *104);* and "'You shall not take vengeance or bear a grudge against your countrymen' (Lev. 19:18)—but you may take vengeance or bear a grudge against a non-Jew" (Sifra ad loc.). Kahane's book presents these and other passages, twisted out of context, as God-given imperatives. It is no wonder that the disciple carried out his master's dictates.

Nevertheless, the massacre would not have taken place had Goldstein not been able to rely on the support of the milieu in which he lived—sympathy manifested by the way in which many residents of Kiryat Arba, including well-known rabbis, reacted to the massacre. Not only did they refuse to condemn the murderer's actions; some lauded him and called him a "martyr" and a "righteous man."

The reactions of these residents of the Jewish suburb of the City of the Patriarchs, most of whom are not shackled by

Kahane's simplistic and satanic doctrines, were based on a halakhic and ideological infrastructure built up over the decades by leading rabbis. This platform continues to provide the settlers with theological backing in their confrontations with Arabs and with successive Israeli governments.

As long ago as 1953, when a retaliatory raid on the village of Kibya[6] resulted in the deaths of some fifty Arab civilians — men, women, and children—Rabbi Shaul Yisraeli, a member of the Chief Rabbinate council, justified the deed: "'The children's death' is considered to be a punishment from Heaven, a situation in which children are certainly punished for the sins of their parents." Some twenty years later this view was seconded by Rabbi Shimon Weiser, who proclaimed: "although in peacetime it is forbidden to kill non-Jews, ... *in wartime it is a mitzvah to kill them.*" The chief chaplain of the Central Command of the Israel Defense Forces, Rabbi Lt. Col. Avraham Avidan published a pamphlet that declared: "In wartime, when Israeli forces are attacking the enemy, they may and in fact are required by halakhah to kill even good civilians, that is, civilians who seem to be good. This was the case about which the Sages said, 'the best among non-Jews—kill!'"

Around the same time Rabbi Yaakov Ariel, today the chief rabbi of Ramat Gan, published an article that enumerated the options he would allow the Arabs of the Land of Israel: they could convert, accept the status of resident aliens, or decide "of their own free will" to emigrate to another country.

Rabbi Zvi Yehuda Kook, the spiritual mentor of Gush Emunim, the movement of right-wing settlers maintained that today the commandment to occupy and settle the Land of the Israel has the same status as the most serious of the negative prohibitions, namely, those against bloodshed, idolatry, and incest: one must allow oneself to be killed rather than transgress them.

Exhortations of this sort by eminent rabbis, expounded in the ostensible name of halakhah and Torah, constitute the ideological basis of Gush Emunim. They are liable to have an influence on every right-wing Torah-observant Jew, as we saw in the settlers' reactions to the Hebron massacre.

But halakhah is pluralistic and provides the settlers with every possibility to turn their backs on those who preach hatred. For example, they might heed Rabbi Abraham Isaac Kook's humane ruling concerning Arabs: "We should say that the Muslims are not idolaters and fall into the category of resident aliens and may be settled in the Land of Israel."

Similarly, the late chief rabbi Yitzhak Isaac Herzog ruled that non-Jews who are not idolaters should not be prevented from settling in the Land of Israel, even though they have not stood before a Jewish religious court and formally accepted the seven Noahide commandments.

In contrast, Rabbi Shlomo Goren, the former chief rabbi, claimed that it is forbidden to evacuate any of the territories, because the Torah commanded us "*lo tahanem*—you shall not let them settle in the Land" and the Sages interpreted this to mean: "*lo titen lanem nanaya bakarka* — you shall not allow the goyim to settle in the Land." Rabbi Goren pronounced: "Evacuating settlements in Judea and Samaria in order to deliver them to the Arabs is a grievous sin against the Torah."

We have seen that halakhic verdicts can have great influence on acts of violence. Yigal Amir, the convicted murderer of Prime Minister Yitzhak Rabin, was apparently influenced by these teachings. The following is a dialogue between Amir and the remanding judge in the magistrates court at the time of his arraignment:

AMIR: There is a *p'sak halakhah* (halakhic verdict) which establishes that it is permitted to kill someone who gives away part of the Eretz Israel. According to the *halakhah*, the moment that a Jew delivers up *(moser)* his people and land into the hand of a gentile, we are obligated to kill him.

JUDGE: What rabbi taught you this halakhah?

AMIR: No one taught this to me. I have studied Talmud all my life … There are *taryag mitzvot* (613 commandments) in the Torah

JUDGE: Have the Ten Commandments been nullified?

AMIR: The Ten Commandments have not been eliminated, but there is a divine command that is higher than thou shalt not murder. That is saving life. It is the same as when you kill the enemy in war there is a higher purpose and therefore it is permitted. If the prime minister declares that he is not responsible for the security of 2 percent of the population (the settlers in the territories) and shakes the hand of the master murder (Arafat) and frees terrorists from prison … he is not my prime minister.[7]

We note that there are two halakhic accusations against the prime minister, which in the eyes of the murderer and those who are like minded, justify his execution. The two capital charges, in their view, are those of *moser* and *rodef*.

The *moser* is one who informs on a Jew or hands him over to Gentiles. Maimonides states that the prohibition of informing or delivering up a Jew to the enemy applies to both the person and his possessions *(Laws of Damage and Destruction* 8; 9-10). What kind of mind is it that would interpret these *halakhot* as applicable to the duly elected head of a sovereign state? Is there any geographical location in the Land of Israel inhabited by any group of individuals, who may decide by fiat that a government treaty with another sovereign party or state is a transgression of *din moser*—the law against handing over a Jew to the enemy.

Is the city of Hebron considered to be a Jewish individual that is in danger of being delivered up to the enemy (as was suggested by Rabbi Goren?) Where in Jewish Law can an individual or even 2 percent of the population claiming to represent the settlers of the territories) decide who is the enemy and who is the *moser*? Is this not the exclusive prerogative a democratically elected government? In such a government is not justice to be dispensed through the duly appointed courts? There is not only a misinterpretation of halakhah, but a distortion of the process of justice where an individual or group unduly take upon themselves to be the prosecutor, judge and executioner.

The late prime minister was accused of being not only a *moser*, but a *rodef* as well. Maimonides defines this criminal as follows: "One who is pursuing after another to kill him, all Jews are obligated to save the pursued individual, even at the cost of the life of the pursuer." Furthermore, the Rambam adds: "If they can save the pursued by wounding one of the limbs of the pursuer, they should do so and not kill the latter." *(Laws of Murder and Preservation of Life* 1:7). One of Amir's fellow students testified that he had asked the head of the yeshiva whether this law of *rodef* is applicable today.

The rabbi did not answer, but pointed instead to the open Talmud volume on his study stand and left the room. The student approached the stand and saw that the *gemara* was open to Tractate Sanhedrin 49a. Here he read the following:

> Then Joab [the late King David's general] was brought before the court and King Solomon cross-examined him. "Why did you kill Abner [King Saul's cousin and commander-in-chief]? [Joab replied: "I was the avenger of the blood of Asahel (Joab's brother, who was killed by Abner]." Solomon interrogated him further: "But Asahel was a pursuer [rodef]! Joab: "Even so, Abner should have saved

himself at the cost of one of this [Asahel's] limbs. Solomon: "Yet perhaps he could not do so." [Rashi Abner was unable to aim precisely to hit one of his limbs]. Joab retorted: "If Abner could aim exactly at the fifth rib [where the gallbladder and liver are located], could he not have aimed at one of his limbs? Thereupon Solomon concluded: "Let's drop the incident of Abner ...."

Thus the Yeshivah students learned the fate of a *rodef* from this Talmudic anecdote.

We have heard that when the accused killer addressed the court trying him for murder, Yigal Amir expounded not only his political motives but also the theological impetus for the crime. "According to halakhah," he intoned, "when a Jew hands over his people and land to the enemy, we must kill him."

Where did the murderer learn this distorted "halakhah"? The rabbis of the various Orthodox educational institutions in which Yigal Amir studied over the years all disavowed responsibility for his views. Rabbi Mordechai Greenberg of the Kerem Be-Yavne yeshiva was quoted to the effect that "I do not believe that he absorbed the ideology behind his act in our yeshiva." Rabbi Moshe Razel, the head of the Higher Institute for Torah at Bar-Ilan University, maintained that Amir and other right-wing students of this institution did not receive any Torah-based guidance that might be interpreted as justifying murder.

Where, then, did Amir derive the loathsome view that a "lofty goal" that is "a Heavenly injunction" may justify violation of the commandment "Thou shalt not murder"? We do know about one particular document that was distributed in some synagogues on the Day of Atonement in 1995 and gleefully read out on television by a member of the extreme right-wing Kahane Chai group. Its heading is *Pulsa Derura* (an Aramaic expression that Rashi glosses as "lashes of fire"). The term appears in several Talmudic legends—for instance, the description of the punishment of the angel Gabriel (BT Yoma 77a—and, in more moderate form, in the responsa literature of the sixteenth through twentieth centuries.[8]

The document in question, however, is neither folktale nor prayer (as it was sometimes described by the media). Rather, influenced by "practical kabbalah" or witchcraft, it is a test of black magic and excommunication, a death-curse directed at a particular person, in this case the late prime minister, as we learn from the text:

> With regard to Yitzhak son of Rosa, known as Rabin, permission is
> given by the destroying angels to send a sword against that wicked
> man. The angels of destruction, who are the emissaries from below,
> have no permission to be merciful to him and forgive him for his
> sins. For this reason, let any good he may have done in this world
> be forgotten … so he may be killed because he misleads the holy
> nation and hands over the Land of Israel to our enemies …

There is no escaping the echo of this monstrous death sentence in the assassin's declaration that it is an obligation to kill a
Jew who hands over his people and land to the enemy. Is this
similarity merely happenstance? Or is this one small tile from the
mosaic of distorted halakhah that underlay this atrocious crime?

We may therefore conclude that the questionable attempts to
give halakhic support to relatively "minor" acts of violence such
as stoning vehicles, wild demonstrations against archaeologists,
and damaging the shops and homes of those who peacefully
carry on their own way of life, can and have escalated into acts
which have catastrophic results.

Israelis have been told to respect the feelings of pious Orthodox Jews. Indeed there is much beauty and wisdom in our
halakhic tradition, which has guided the people of Israel and
kept them alive through the millennia. But when these words are
twisted and distorted and lead to impious violent action, they
can be very dangerous. All teachers of Torah should remember
the stern warning of Abtalion, the teacher of Hillel and Shammai:
"Sages, give heed to your words, lest you incur the penalty of
exile to a place of evil waters, and the disciples that come after
you drink thereof and die, and the name of Heaven will be profaned" (Mishnah Avot 1:11).[9]

Notes

1. See *Yedioth Ahronoth*, March 11, 1974.
2. *Amudim, The Journal of the Religious Kibbutz Movement* (Elul, 5739) (1979): 417; emphasis in the original.
3. See Israel Meir Kagan, *Mishnah Berurah* 262:9.
4 See Hayyim Joseph David Axulai, *Sefer Avodat Hakodesh*, Chapter 4, 152, p. 30b.
5. See Abraham Isaac Hakohen Kook, *Lights of Repentance*, Chapter 17, 3, pp. 159-60.
6. "At 9:30 p.m. on 14 October (1953), soldiers from Unit 101 and an IDF paratroop unit crossed the border and attacked the village of Kibya ... Houses were blown up during the operation and dozens of people were killed or wounded. Reports on the number of slain ranged from 43 to 56 persons .... The raid was conducted after several incidents in which infiltrators from Jordan had attacked Israeli citizens, culminating in the murders in Yahud, in which Arab infiltrators threw a grenade through an open window into a house, killing a mother and her two children, aged 1 and 3." *(Documents on the Foreign Policy of Israel*, Vol. 8 (Jerusalem, 1995), p. 357).
7. *Ha'aretz*, November 6, 1995. Shimon Weiser, "Purity of Arms: An Exchange of Letters," *Niv Hamidrashiyah* 11: 29-30 (emphasis in the original).
8. For example, *Responsa Be'er Sheva* 48 (sixteenth century); Moses Sofer, *Responsa hatam Sofer* 5, 124 and 7, 35 (nineteenth century). See also my article "Reshut mi'malakhei Ha'habalah" *Ha'aretz*, November 14, 1995.
9. This essay is based in part on the author's book *Evolving Halakhah* (Vermont, 1999).

Part Two

❖   ❖   ❖

SELECTED REFORM RESPONSA

These responsa on crime and punishment are a representative selection from more than one thousand American Reform responsa published in the twentieth century. We are grateful to the Central Conference of American Rabbis and the Hebrew Union College Press for permission to reproduce them.

Professional Secrecy and an Illegal Act

Contemporary American Reform Responsa (New York, 1987), #4

Walter Jacob

QUESTION: A lawyer has discovered that a fellow attorney is providing a client with advice which will lead to an illegal act and the possibility of considerable financial loss. The lawyer asking the question has gained this information in a confidential relationship. Should he break that confidence and inform the client in question?

ANSWER: It is clear that privacy and information gained as part of a professional relationship can generally not be divulged (Lev. 19.16 *Yad* Hil. Deot 7), yet this prohibition is not absolute. For example, if knowledge of certain medical information might change a marriage, such information should be presented (Israel Kagan, *Hofetz Haym,* Hil. Rekhilut 9). The decision is based upon the principal of the "need to know." Such facts must not be given lightly or simply to complete existing information or for any personal gain. If such information would lead to the protection of lives or prevent personal injury and financial loss, it must be divulged in accordance with the Biblical injunction of Leviticus, "You shall not stand idly by the blood of your neighbor" (Lev. 19.16). If an individual's life is endangered, immediate action to remove that danger must be undertaken. This was also the interpretation provided for our verse by tradition (San. 73b; *Yad* Hil. Rotzeah 1.13 f, 15; 4.16; Hil. San. 2.4, 5, 12; *Shulhan Arukh, Hoshen Mishpat* 425.10, 426.1). Maimonides considered it necessary to move in this direction in cases of idolatry *(Yad* Hil. A. Z. 5.4) and rape *(Yad* Hil. Naarah 3.1). This would apply, however, only if the client's life is endangered; that is not the case here.

Maimonides and some others go further through the exegesis of another verse from Leviticus (19.14), "Thou shalt not place a stumbling block before the blind." This would include reporting someone who provides incorrect advice which might lead to criminal acts or to a considerable financial loss *(Yad* Hil. Rotzeah 12.4; Jakob Breish, *Helkat Yaaqov* III 136; Elijah of Vilna, *Biur Hagra,* Yoreh Deah 295.2; Joshua Falk, *Peri Megadim,* Orah Hayim 443.5, 444.6). We must also ask about the status of attorneys in Jewish law. Generally, attorneys are not used in the traditional Jewish courts, although they have sometimes been appointed by the court (Ribash *Responsa* #235; Meir of Rothenburg *Responsa* #357). In other words, the litigants and the witnesses are present in person (M. Mak 1.9; *Yad* Hil. San. 21.8). Exceptions are only made when the individual involved is unavoidably absent or is too timid to defend himself *(Tos.* to Shev. 31a; *Tur Hoshen Mishpat* 123.16; also Bet Yosef).

When an attorney is appointed, the fiction is created that he acts entirely on his own behalf. He, therefore, has complete power of attorney for the defendant (B. K. 70a; *Yad* Hil. Sheluhin Veshutafin 3.7; *Shulkhan Arukh Hoshen Mishpat* 122-123; *Arukh Hashulhan Hoshen Mishpat* 124).

There was, in other words, a reluctance to use attorneys, but by the late Middle Ages, they have been admitted to court, especially if the parties involved were present and their reaction could be watched. Such attorneys are paid by a fee for their services (Rif, *Responsa* #157; Rashba, *Responsa* II #393, III #141, V #287, etc.).

An attorney, therefore, acts as an agent and the laws of the agency apply to him. There is a legal presumption that an agent properly performs the duties assigned to him (Git. 64a); any agent is considered to have been appointed by a client to benefit and not to harm him (Kid. 42b). In this instance, the attorney might be considered akin to both an agent and an expert. Experts who are paid for their advice are liable if their opinion proves to be wrong (B. K. 99bff; Simon ben Zemah of Duran, *Responsa* II, #174).

As the lawyer in question has not been ethical and has provided improper guidance to his client, it is the duty of the attorney to inform the Bar Association or other appropriate authorities of the misconduct which he suspects. This course of action should be followed in criminal and civil procedures.

Damages for a Physician's Error

Contemporary American Reform Responsa (New York, 1987), #75

Walter Jacob

QUESTION: An elderly woman suffering from a variety of ailments was mistakenly given an excessive dosage of a drug. This led to her serious rapid deterioration and hastened her death. The physician in question immediately admitted his error and did everything possible to rectify it. Is the family entitled to damages on moral and ethical grounds? Should this course be pursued to make the doctor more careful in the future? (M. M., Pittsburgh, Pennsylvania)

ANSWER: The Talmud dealt with the general problem of a physician's liability while healing the sick. The Talmud considered the task of healing a *mitzvah* and not interference with God's intentions [as He may have sent the disease] (B. K. 85a; *Bet Josef* to *Tur* Yoreh Deah 336). It was a person's duty to seek the best physician in case of illness (Shab. 32a). Furthermore, it was permitted to violate all shabbat and ritual laws to save a human life (Yoma 85b; *Shulhan Arukh* Orah Hayim 329.3). If the physician failed and the patient died, he is free from liability as long as the remedies were tried in good faith (*Tosefta* Git. 4.6). This *Tosefta* discussed other situations of inadvertent injury incurred while performing a *mitzvah*. As long as the injury is inadvertent, no liability is incurred. The traditional statements are very specific about the physician's responsibility and free him from general liability for unintentional harm. Without such assurance it would be impossible for a physician to practice (David Pardons J. Preuss, *Biblical and Talmudic Medicine*, p. 28). It is, of course, assumed that the physician has been trained and properly licensed (Nachmanides; *Torat Ha-adam* 12b; Simon ben Zemah of Duran, *Responsa*, Vol. 3; *Tur* Yoreh Deah 336; *Shulhan Arukh* Yoreh Deah 336; Eliezer Waldenberg, *Tzitz Eliezer*, Vol. 5, #23).

When, however, the physician has clearly made a mistake, then he is liable for the same damages as anyone engaged in other professional or commercial transactions (Tosefta 8. K. 9.11). The general laws of liability apply here. The surviving family is entitled to damages on moral and ethical grounds and should pursue this course of action. The physician may well be willing to assume this obligation in keeping with tradition.

Suing the Rabbi

Questions and Reform Jewish Answers (New York, 1992), #235

Walter Jacob

QUESTION: A rabbi who does a considerable amount of counseling has asked whether it is necessary to purchase malpractice insurance. What, according to tradition, is the range of liability? (Walter Rosenthal, Trenton New Jersey)

ANSWER: We are going to look at this matter with the understanding that the rabbi in question is not a licensed therapist and so would do counseling as part of ordinary congregational responsibility and not in the special capacity of a therapist. Such cases would be akin to the responsibility of a physician which has been discussed previously (W. Jacob, *Contemporary American Reform Responsa* # 75).

This entire area has been treated thoroughly in American secular legal literature; it is the general desire of the courts to remain out of this area, as it is very difficult for them to establish the parameters of training and appropriate religious conduct for so many religious groups and sects (Funston, "Made out of Whole Cloth—A Constitutional Analysis of the Clergy Malpractice Concept," *Georgia Western Law Review*, Vol 10, pp. 507ff; McMenamin *The Jurist*, Vol 45, pp. 275ff etc).

We are not concerned with the judicial function of the rabbi and possible errors which might take place in the exercise of that function (*Shulhan Arukh Hoshen Mishpat* 25 and commentaries), but rather with the general area of responsibility through counseling.

The rabbi would be liable if there was gross neglect, for then he/she would be violating the Biblical statement "Do not place a stumbling block before the blind" (Lev 19.14). However, the later Talmudic development of the law of torts is rather confused; we have two concepts, *garmi* which includes those actions directly responsible for damage, and *gerama or* matters in which the action is indirect *(Encyclopedia Talmudit* Vol 6; Ramban *Dina Degarmi; Shulhan Arukh Hoshen Mishpat* 386). The general rule which we may abstract from the many cases cited in the literature is as follows: If the individual in question is an expert and the advice which is followed is based upon his expertise, then he would be liable. As for example, a coin appraiser who has been shown a coin and has declared it good, but subsequently it was discovered to be bad coinage. If he has been paid for his advice, then he is liable. If he has not been paid, then he is not liable. On the other hand, if he is not an absolute expert, but the individual who came stated that he was relying on this person's opinion alone, then he is also liable *(Yad* Hil. Shirut.5). We can see from this that the matters which are involved are: (a) The expert status; (b) the exchange of money for the advice and evaluation; (c) the agreement between the individuals that this person is the only one to be asked for advice.

In the case of counseling ordinarily done by rabbis, there is no exchange of funds. The rabbi makes no pretense to being an expert in the field. In addition to that, a rabbi would and should not permit himself/herself to be placed in a position of being the only person consulted, particularly in a difficult matter. It is our common practice to refer difficult matters onward and even in other counseling situations to provide only tentative advice. Furthermore, following the rabbinic advice is entirely voluntary. This is not like a business transaction in which the paths are much clearer; it involves a great many areas: (a) theological issues; (b) to what extent was the party being counseled completely forthcoming; (c) was there an opportunity to see other parties or to gather additional information about this matter, (d) the party seeking counseling remains completely independent and may accept or reject the advice. From a traditional point of view, therefore, there is little or no ground for a suit to be brought against a rabbi as the counseling situation leaves so many areas open.

Malpractice Suits Against Rabbis

Today's Reform Responsa (Cincinnati, 1990), #50

Solomon B. Freehof

QUESTION: The Church Mutual Insurance Company founded by Lutheran ministers in 1897 has recently begun to sell malpractice insurance to ministers. This is an innovation and is based upon reports that there have been suits for malpractice when the minister gave wrong advice in counseling. However, a careful study of the situation revealed that, at the very most, there were only two such suits in the country. So it has been charged that the whole situation must have been blown up in order to sell insurance. However, nowadays when people are, as one person interviewed described it, "sue crazy," and when malpractice suits have already multiplied against doctors, lawyers and accountants, this type of suit against ministers may indeed increase. Therefore the question now asked is: To what extent, on the basis of Jewish tradition, is a rabbi to be held liable for harm coming from wrong advice that he had given. The question is still theoretical and, it is hoped, may never become practical, but it is worth preliminary investigation from the point of view of tradition. (Asked by Rabbi Lawrence J. Goldmark, La Mirada, California.)

ANSWER: In one of the suits the minister's lawyer said that the suit is an anti-constitutional interference with the separation of church and state. This may well be argued on the ground that while lawyers and doctors may not practice unless they are licensed by the state, ministers are not licensed by the state, but are licensed by their denomination. The only authorization which the state gives to the minister is that if he is already accepted by the church as a minister, the state then gives him the right to officiate at marriage, for the laws governing marriage are state laws. Yet even in the case of marriage, in which the state has authority over the work of the minister, is it at all conceivable that the minister could justly be sued for malpractice when a marriage at which he had officiated turns into a tragic mismatch? When one sees what a flood of suits could start in this all-too-frequent situation, it is clear that the courts cannot permit such suits. However, in all other activities of the minister except marriage, the state has no authority. Nevertheless, the minister does a great deal of counseling and in this activity, he often overlaps the work of the psychiatrist who *is* a professional, licensed by the state and subject in a suit to punishment by the state. Therefore, when the minister in his counseling does psychiatric work, it is there that there would be the chief ground for possible malpractice suits.

Therefore, our specific question here is: To what extent does Jewish tradition hold a rabbi liable for harm resulting from his counsel? Actually there is some sort of liability, due to the historic function of the rabbi as judge. If a rabbi is part of a court (a *bet din*) in the case of some financial dispute and gives a wrong decision, then, if this decision cannot be reversed when the harm due to the mistake has already been done, there are circumstances in which the judge (i.e., the rabbi) must make up for the damage from his own property (*Hoshen Mishpat* 25). Therefore we would say that if some Jewish businessman would bring a case before a *bet din* of rabbis and a wrong decision was given, there are indeed, in Jewish law, certain circumstances under which the rabbi is liable to make restitution. But, even so, the businessman would not need to institute a malpractice suit in the civil courts, since Jewish law under which the cam was heard already provides for the restitution. But actually this situation is rare. Few people bring their business disputes nowadays to a *bet din* and if they do, then, considering the long and detailed development of Jewish law, there is almost no likelihood of such liability being incurred by the rabbi-judge.

The only potential cases in which a modern malpractice suit is likely to occur is in the field of family or personal counseling. We must therefore ask: Is such counseling an inherent function of the rabbi? It must be understood at the outset that personal and family counseling is indeed an essential part of the work of the Christian ministry. At the very beginning of the Christian ministry, Jesus said to disciples: Feed my sheep. (John 21:16). Since that beginning, the guidance of each individual Christian was a central responsibility of the pastor, whose very title means "the shepherd." The church has a name for this individual counseling. It is an historic name for an historic function, *cura animarum* (the healing of the spirit). In the Lutheran Church the term used is *Seelensorge*. The Latin and German terms could be translated into the Greek as "psychiatry." The "healing of souls" is the essential task of the Christian minister. So if a Christian minister errs in his counseling, one could well argue (in a suit) that he has made a professional error, as a doctor who gives the wrong medicine has made a professional error.

This personal guidance has never been an essential part of the rabbi's task. He was, as mentioned above, the judge, but primarily he was the teacher. People would, of course, come to him for advice, as they would to any other person whom they respected as intelligent. But giving the advice was not an essential or required part of his profession. He is a teacher, not a pastor, a shepherd of the flock.

Of course in recent years counseling as a practice has developed among our rabbis. This is understandable. Partly it is due to the influence of the Christian environment and partially because in these confused and troubled times people increasingly come to the rabbi for advice. But unlike the Christian minister, the rabbi is not required by his profession to give advice in every situation. He may, if it seems proper to him, refuse to interfere. For it must be understood that to the extent that rabbis follow the practice of Christian clergy and give psychiatric advice, they do run the risk of such malpractice suits.

This at least we can say in defense of the rabbi in such a suit. We share the Christian defense of the separation of church and state, but we also have the additional defense that such counseling is not a required part of the rabbinical profession and therefore, such mistakes cannot be ascribed to professional failure. It is not malpractice on our part, because counseling is not the required practice of the rabbinical profession. It is simply advice given by one person to another.

What we can learn from the threat of such suits for which this clerical insurance company is now selling insurance, is that we should be careful in our counseling not to infringe upon the work of a psychiatrist. We must always remember and always to remember that while we do practice counseling when necessary, this counseling is not an essential part of the traditional function of the rabbinate, and that we will not be neglectful of our rabbinical duty if in certain cases we say "This situation is not one in which I can be of help."

Confidential Information

Contemporary American Reform Responsa (New York), #5

Walter Jacob

QUESTION: A rabbi has been told by one of his congregants that she suffers from a rare disorder which may kill her prematurely. The congregant now intends to be married. The woman in question has stated clearly that she will commit suicide if the information is divulged to her fiancé. Is it the rabbi's duty to inform the groom or should the information given in a confidential manner be kept secret by the rabbi?

ANSWER: The biblical prohibition against "being a tale bearer" is quite precise (Lev. 19.16), even when the information is true and accurate *(Yad* Hil. Deot. 7.2). However, in this case this biblical citation is opposed by others in the same chapter of Leviticus, "You shall not place a stumbling block before the blind" (Lev. 19.14). In other words, one must prevent someone from committing a sin or placing themselves in a position of personal or financial loss *(Had* Hil. Rotzeah 12.4, 1.13). Nor should "one stand idly by the blood of your neighbor" (Lev. 19.16). This has been interpreted to indicate that one should do everything possible to protect life and property from injury directly or indirectly, including providing information *(Yad* Hil. Rotzeah 1.13 *Shulhan Arukh Hoshen Mishpat* 426.1).

Hafetz Hayim (Israel Meir Kagan) argued vigorously for disclosure in a case specifically like this one especially as this may be a major factor in the prospective marriage and lack of such information may endanger the stability of the marriage in the future. Furthermore, in this instance, we are dealing with a life-threatening situation and not a vague problem which need not be revealed *(Sefer Hafetz Hayim* Hil. Rehilut #9).

In analogous situations involving physicians, there is some difference of opinion whether a doctor should volunteer or can be compelled to provide such information, but that is only because it may be contrary to the Hippocratic Oath. Most authorities feel that physicians may be forced to testify (Eliezer Waldenberg, *Tzitz Eliezer,* 13 #81; Jacob Breish, *Helkat Ya-nkov 3,* 136). However, Barukh Rakover argues to the contrary and feels that a physician is bound by the oath *(Noam,* Vol. 2). A rabbi, however, would be duty-bound to divulge the information he possesses.

In this specific instance, the rabbi must weigh the danger of the woman committing suicide against the problem of not providing adequate information to the fiancé. The quotation "do not stand idly by the blood of your neighbor" here weighs heavily on the side of the woman (Lev. 19.16). If the rabbi is convinced that her threat of suicide is real, he may *not* divulge the information.

❖   ❖   ❖

Testimony Against a Family Member

American Reform Responsa (New York, 1983), #170

Walter Jacob

QUESTION: Does a prisoner in a federal correction institution have the right to refuse testimony in a case which involves his father and other members of the family? What is the attitude of Jewish law in this matter? (Rabbi Stanley J. Garfein, Tallahassee, Florida)

ANSWER: The principle that governs all cases of the laws of the land in which we live is, of course, "dina d' malkhuta ("The law of the land is the law"). This talmudic principle has been applied in all matters except those connected with Jewish family law (i.e., marriage and divorce), and even in that area the decision of the Napoleonic Sanhedrin of 1806 gave civil law priority over Jewish law. This principle has been attributed by the Talmud to Samuel of the third century (Git. 10b; B.K. 113a; Ned. 28a; B.B. 54b; *Shulhan Arukh, Hoshen Mishpat* 369.6). Of course, in the Middle Ages Jewish communities were often autonomous and used the Jewish legal systems to govern other communities. The question arose only when there was a conflict between a Jew and a non-Jew, or when a Jew chose to take his case to a non-Jewish court, something that was decried by the Jewish authorities.

The earliest record of a Jew handing a Jewish criminal who had injured non-Jews to a gentile court came from the Gaonic period (700–1000 C.E.; J. Mueller, *Mafteah*, p. 182). The responsa literature contains numerous examples of Jews testifying in non-Jewish courts and doing so willingly when the law of the land demanded it.

The codes summarize various other considerations. Clearly, one may testify to save oneself if punishment is threatened; then one is *moser be-ones*, and should testify before a non Jewish court (*Tur, Hoshen Mishpat* 388; *Shulhan Arukh, Ch.M.* 388.8ff; *Yad, Hil.* Chovel 8.2).

Furthermore, if the withholding of testimony will harm the community, then handing such an individual over to the government, as well as testimony, is mandatory (Isserles to *Shulhan Arukh, Hoshen Mishpat* 388.11). Testimony in criminal cases is every witness' obligation (Lev. 5:1; B.K. 55b), while in civil cases a witness may wait until summoned (*Shulhan Arukh, Ch.M.* 28.1). A witness must possess personal knowledge of the events (Isserles to *Shulhan Arukh, Ch.M.* 19, 28.1).

In our instance, it seems that we are not dealing with a government demand for testimony—as that would certainly have to be met—but with a request to volunteer testimony. The decision then rests in the hands of the individual involved.

He may wish to be guided by the principles surrounding family witnesses in a purely Jewish court. Members of the immediate family are not eligible to act as witnesses and are disqualified. The tradition interpreted the statement of Deuteronomy 24:16 that parents should not be put to death for their children or children for their parents as a prohibition against parents testifying against children or children against parents (San. 27b; *Sifrei Deut.* 280). The Mishna expanded this list of disqualified relatives considerably so that it included father, brother, uncle, brother-in-law, stepfather, father-in-law, their sons, and sons-in-law (San. 3.4). Later the rule was extended still further to include nephews and first cousins (*Yad, Hil.* Edut 12.3; *Shulhan Arukh, Hoshen Mishpat* 33.2).

A husband was disqualified in cases involving his wife (*Yad, Hil.* Edut 13.6; *Shulhan Arukh, Hoshen Mishpat* 33.3). Testimony from the individuals listed above for or against the accused was not permitted in court, and it did not matter whether these relatives retained any ties with the accused or not (_Yad_, Hil. Edut 13.6; _Shulhan Arukh, Hoshen Mishpat_ 33.3).

Jewish tradition, therefore, very clearly eliminated all relatives from this kind of judicial involvement in contrast to other legal systems. The ancient Greek legal system had no qualms about the testimony of relatives (W. Smith, _A Dictionary of Greek and Roman Antiquities_, p. 626). In Rome, such testimony was not excluded, but it was given little weight. In English common law, relatives, except husband and wife, may testify against or for each other (H. Roscoe, _A Digest of the Law of Evidence_, pp. 112ff).

It is clear, therefore, that from the point of view of a Jewish court, such an individual should not testify against any member of his family, but he must testify (1) if a criminal act endangers the community, or (2) if the law of the land demands such testimony in accordance with the principle "_dina d'malkhuta dina_" this may restrain bitter family feelings which might arise from such circumstances (Gulak, _Hamishpat Ha-Ivri_ IV.1).

❖   ❖   ❖

Informing on Others in Criminal Activities

Contemporary American Reform Responsa #6 (New York, 1987)

Walter Jacob

QUESTION: A prisoner has asked whether he is, according to Jewish law, duty-bound to inform on others in criminal matters with which he is charged. This will probably be part of "plea bargaining." What is his duty according to our tradition? (Rabbi W. J. Leffler, Lexington, Kentucky)

ANSWER: Jewish tradition states that information which, if withheld, would harm individuals or the community, either through criminal activity or considerable financial loss, must be presented. This is based on a Biblical statement (Lev. 19.16) as well as later authorities *(Yad Hil.* Rotzeah 1.13; *Shulhan Arukh Hoshen Mishpat* 426.1; Elijah of Vilna *Biur Hagra, Hoshen Mishpat* 425.20; Isserles to *Shulhan Arukh Hoshen Mishpat* 388.11). Furthermore, in a criminal case every witness is obligated to testify if he possesses personal knowledge of the events (Lev. 5.1; B. K. 55b; Isserles to *Shulhan Arukh Hoshen Mishpat* 28.1).

It is also clear that a person is obligated to testify before a Jewish or non-Jewish court in order to save himself from threatened punishment. Under such circumstances, one is *moser beones (Tur Hoshen Mishpat* 388; *Shulhan Arukh Hoshen Mishpat* 388.8ff; *Yad* Hil. Hovel 8.2). We should note that there is no problem of testifying before a non Jewish court. We have records of a Jewish community handing a Jewish criminal who had injured a non-Jew to a gentile court as early as the Gaonic Period (700-1000 C.E.; J. Mueller, *Mafteah,* p. 182).

It is quite clear, therefore, that Jewish law requires an individual to testify and that there is no reason to hesitate.

❖   ❖   ❖

Electronic Eavesdropping and Jewish Law

Reform Responsa for Our Time (Cincinnati, 1977), #6

Solomon B. Freehof

QUESTION: May information obtained through electronic eavesdropping be used as evidence in Jewish law? (Asked by Rabbi Richard F. Steinbrink, Saint Louis, Missouri)

ANSWER: Jewish law is basically religious (canon) law, and therefore it is not surprising that many of its rules are widely different from those governing secular legal systems. Thus, the Jewish laws governing the eligibility of witnesses and the admissibility of evidence are much more severely limited than those of secular legal systems. For example, a gentile is not eligible as a witness in a Jewish court (except in the special case of freeing a woman for remarriage when her husband has disappeared, *aguna*). Also, a child may not be a witness, nor a woman, nor a gambler, nor may any man testify in behalf of a near relative.

Since the laws of evidence in Jewish courts are so different from those governing secular courts, it would seem meaningless to draw any analogies between the two on any matter involving the rules governing witnesses or admissible evidence. Yet such a question *can* be meaningful if we go beyond the actual rules (or certain rules) of evidence and try to reach the ethical basis upon which they rest. In this deeper sense, the older (Jewish) system may give some moral guidance in some of the newer legal problems. This is surely the meaning of the question here. What really is asked is: According to the *ethical* standards underlying Jewish legal procedure, would it be deemed morally right to use a tape obtained by electronic eavesdropping as evidence in a secular court case?

Of course, it is obvious that classic Jewish law could not possibly know of the modern devices whereby voices recorded on a tape can be repeated in the hearing of the court, and used thus as testimony of guilt or of financial obligation. Furthermore, as has been stated, Jewish law as to testimony is extremely strict in defense of the innocent, or the possibly innocent, and thus reveals an especially high ethical standard. Then let us assume that the sound of the voice from the tape may be considered the same as the voice of a witness testifying. Would such a witness be accepted as competent in Jewish law even though the tape is not a living witness?

First as to criminal law, even if it were accepted as a witness (assuming that for the moment), it would not be *sufficient* testimony, because in Jewish criminal law there must be two witnesses together in the court at the same time, both testifying to having observed the same crime at the same time. So, along with the tape, there would have to be a living witness as the second witness, and he would have to testify that he has personal knowledge through his own senses of the same crime to which the tape attests. The tape alone could not be admissible because we would not have here independent witnesses. If it were possible for a living witness to attest the alleged fact, it is not likely that there would also be need of surreptitious eavesdropping. But at all events, the tape, even if it *were* acceptable as a witness, is invalid in Jewish criminal law unless there is another witness who can testify of his own knowledge to the same facts at the same time.

With regard to civil law, disputes as to debts, etc., the two witnesses do not need to have observed the facts in dispute simultaneously. However, there are certain definite restrictions to testimony, other than those mentioned above, which are relevant to our question. The crucial fact in Jewish legal testimony is that the witnesses must hear the words of the judges and the judges' warnings against false testimony, and they must submit to cross-examination by the judges (this is *always* the rule in criminal cases, and in case of doubt also in civil cases). It is for this reason that the preponderant weight of Jewish law is against testimony in writing (i.e., by affidavit); see Rashi to *Gittin* 71a). The *Tur* (in *Hoshen Mishpat 28)* cites Rashi's opinion, but adds that Rabbenu Tam permitted written testimony. However the *Shulhan Arukh* (ibid.) upholds the general rule that only *oral* testimony is acceptable. It is because the witnesses must hear the warning of the judges and accept cross-examination that deaf-mutes are considered incompetent to serve as witnesses in a Jewish court (see *Hoshen Mishpat 35:* 1 1 and also the *Tur*; see also Maimonides in *Yad, Hil. Edut, IX. 9).* Such restrictions are all based upon the Talmud in *Gittin* 71a, where certain rights are assured to deaf-mutes with regard to marriage and divorce, but they may not testify against someone else, since Scripture in Deuteronomy 17:6 says that only "from the *mouth* of the witnesses" can a man be condemned. There are, by the way, certain alleviations to this rule; for example, a woman who is an *agunah* may be freed from her unhappy state through the testimony of a deaf-mute. But this is testimony to help her and is, of course, a special case. In general, the law in all the Codes based on this Talmudic passage is that a deaf-mute is not a competent witness because he cannot hear the warnings of the judges or be subjected effectively to cross-examination.

The moral basis of this restriction is clear enough. No man can be justly condemned unless the witnesses and their testimony can be carefully scrutinized and weighed. For similar reasons (that the witness must hear the judge and may be cross-examined), only oral testimony (but not written testimony), according to most authorities, is admissible. This certainly applies to the admissibility of an electronic tape. At best it is written rather than oral testimony. At worst it is equivalent to a deaf-mute because it cannot be questioned and it cannot be warned. If a living witness cunningly concocts a false testimony, he can be questioned and perhaps trapped in his deceit. But if a tape is cleverly faked, the tape itself is like a deaf-mute and cannot be spoken to.

Therefore one may say that by the moral high standards of Jewish court testimony, a tape cannot be accepted as a witness or as testimony.

Addendum

I consulted Eugene B. Strassburger, a prominent lawyer, and asked him whether any of the objections to electronic eavesdropping in American law are based upon reasonings analogous to those in the Jewish legal tradition. He answered that he has not seen a case where objection was made on the grounds (mentioned in the responsum) that the tape could not be cross-examined. He mentioned, however, the right of the people to be secure in their houses (i.e., privacy). Then he continued as follows: "The Fifth Amendment to the Constitution provides: 'No person ... shall be compelled in any criminal case to be a witness against himself.' Electronic devices by which a defendant in a criminal case is heard to make a statement against himself violate this amendment."

There are, indeed, similar regulations in Jewish law defending the privacy of private premises. One may not make a window overlooking a neighbor's court. The neighbor can object on the basis of *hezek r'iah* ("the damage of looking"), i.e., invasion of privacy (*Hoshen Mishpat* 154:6 ff., Maimonides, *Yad, Hilchot Shehenim* VII).

But more significant in Jewish law is the prohibition against a man being compelled to incriminate himself. The Talmud, in *Yevamos* 25b, speaks of a man's relatives being ineligible as witnesses, and then says: "A man is considered to be his own relative and therefore may not declare himself to be evil, or criminal." See Rashi to the passage in which he says: "A man may confess to a debt, but he may not make any confession against himself in criminal law." So, too, Maimonides in *Yad*, *Edus* XII, 2. In fact, Jewish law seems to be even stricter than general law in this matter. Not only may he not be compelled to incriminate himself, but he may not incriminate himself even of his own free will. He is simply ineligible as a witness (even if voluntarily) against himself. Certainly by the electronic tape he is, as Mr. Strassburger says, made to incriminate himself. This is against Jewish law, as it is against American law.

❖ ❖ ❖

Disinterment for Legal Evidence

Contemporary American Reform Responsa (New York, 1987), #110

Walter Jacob

QUESTION: May the body of a young person who was murdered be disinterred after a number of years have passed? New evidence has arisen, and it is the contention of the attorney representing the husband of the person who was convicted of murder that this disinterment will provide additional clues about the real killer. (H. B., Massachusetts)

ANSWER: This sad inquiry actually contains three separate questions. First, we must ask about criminal procedures, especially in cases which might lead to the death penalty. How far can we go to obtain evidence? Secondly, we must turn to the general question of disinterment, and finally, to that of autopsy.

It is clear from the Mishnah (Makot, Sanhedrin) that every precaution was taken in the case of capital offenses. The accused was provided with all conceivable opportunities to prove his innocence, and all possible evidence had to be examined. He had to be specifically warned by two witnesses (M. Makot 9.6), etc. A court of twenty-three had to be used (M. San. 4.1). Akiba and others sought to eliminate the death sentence entirely (M. Makot

10.6), This Talmudic line of reasoning made it very difficult to execute anyone. The crime and sentence were publicly announced with a plea for evidence which might prove the accused's innocence. Furthermore, an elaborate communications system was arranged between the courtroom and the place of execution so that any new evidence, even at the last minute, could prevent the execution (M. San. 6.1 ff). As our case is a capital offense, the statements and the intent of tradition apply. These indicate that in order to save the life, or to prevent an error in judgment in a capital offense, every effort to gain evidence on behalf of the accused must be undertaken.

Now let us turn to exhumation. Disinterment is not undertaken lightly in Jewish tradition. The prohibition rests upon a talmudic incident in which disinterment was suggested in order to establish whether the deceased was a child or an adult, and thereby settle a quarrel over property rights. In that instance, it was disallowed (B. B. 155a), because Akiba felt that the dead should not be disturbed. But that was not a capital case. Disinterment has also been prohibited in almost all instances with the exception of the following: a) in order to re-inter in the land of Israel; b) in order to reinter in a family plot, especially if the deceased died away from the city in which he normally resided; and c) in those instances in which the grave was threatened by hostile individuals or by an unforeseen natural event (*Shulhan Arukh* Yoreh Deah 363.1ff).

Whenever burial has taken place in a coffin, rather than merely in shrouds, disinterment has been more readily acceptable as the dead are disturbed less. In our case we are not dealing with the usual cases of disinterment, but with a more serious reason. In view of the intensive search for evidence in all capital cases, disinterment should be permitted in this instance.

Each cemetery has its own regulations, and every effort should be made to abide by them. However, in this instance, as an individual's freedom is at stake, disinterment should be encouraged.

Autopsy has been thoroughly discussed by J. Z. Lauterbach (W. Jacob, *American Reform Responsa*, #82) and S. B. Freehof (*Reform Jewish Practice*, vol. 1, [Pittsburgh PA.], pp. 115ff). As this autopsy will be of immediate benefit in a criminal case, even the more hesitant traditional authorities would permit it.

❖   ❖   ❖

Insanity in Criminal Cases

Contemporary American Reform Responsa (New York, 1987), #7

Walter Jacob

QUESTION: Are there rabbinic opinions on insanity as a defense in a criminal trial? What is the status of the insane in criminal matters? (A. Adelstone, Flushing, New York)

ANSWER: When the Mishnah and the discussed individuals of limited ability, they frequently used the phrase *heresh shoteh vegatan*—the deaf, the insane and the minor; insanity included any serious mental imbalance. No one in these categories may be punished for their offenses, and they are considered to have limited legal liability (M. Erub. 3.2; R. H. 3.8; Meg. 2.4; Hag. 1.1; Git. 2.5, 5.8; B. K. 4.4, 5.6, 6.4, 8.4, etc.). The later Jewish codes continue this classification. The insane are not considered responsible for injuries to others, though others who assault them are liable for the usual punishments (M. B. K. 8.4, 87a; *Yad* Hil. Hovel 24.20; *Shulhan Arukh Hoshen Mishpat* 424.8). However, if the individual has lucid moments, in other words, if insanity is temporary, then he is considered responsible *(Yad* Hil. Mekh. 29; *Shulhan Arukh Hoshen Mishpat* 235.23). If the rights or the estate of persons of unsound mind need to be defended, the court appoints an administrator *(epitropos)* who looks after their interests. They are not entitled to damages in cases of insult or defamation of character (B. K. 86b; *Yad* Hil. Hovel 3.4; *Shulhan Arukh Hoshen Mishpat* 300.27).

The status of the insane in rabbinic literature is, therefore, clear. The discussion of the insane in the later responsa deals almost exclusively with problems of engagement, marriage. divorce or inheritance. Two problems remain for our discussion. How is insanity defined by rabbinic literature? What is temporary lucidity?

The Talmud attempted to define the insane as one "who wanders alone at night and spends the night in the cemetery and tears his garments" (Hag. 3b). This definition was immediately challenged by authorities on the same page, and no resolution was achieved. Others defined insanity to include individuals who were self-destructive or eccentric (Git. 78a; J. Ter. 40b). It was ultimately left to the judges to assess the situation and make a judgement according to the evidence in each case *(Yad* Hil. Edut. 9.9). In order to assure an appropriate decision, the judges were required to possess some knowledge of all the sciences, including medicine *(Yad* Hil. San. 2.1).

Those temporarily insane are not considered liable for acts performed during periods of insanity. However, during times of lucidity, they are liable and could also act as witnesses *(Tos.* Ter. 1.3; J. Ter. 40b; B. B. 128a; *Yad* Hil. Mekh. *29; Shulhan Arukh Hoshen Mishpat* 235.23). The court must decide whether an act has been committed in a period of insanity or lucidity. Furthermore, an individual so intoxicated as to be totally unaware of his actions is considered temporarily insane, and is treated accordingly by the court (Er. 75a; *Yad* Hil. Ishut 4.18). The cases cited in the responsa literature, however, deal with betrothal and marriage, not criminal acts.

Although some guidelines have been mentioned, they are vague and the decision of temporary insanity is left to the court. Individuals who are considered totally insane are not liable for any act which they may commit.

❖   ❖   ❖

Unknown Defect in Building Material

Contemporary American Reform Responsa (New York, 1987), #11

Walter Jacob

QUESTION: Our sanctuary and social hall contain asbestos tiles in their ceilings. The congregation is planning on removing them. At the last board meeting a directive was passed instructing our legal committee to file proceedings against an asbestos manufacturer. Is it moral to bring a liability suit against a manufacturer who was unaware of the potential health hazard of his product when it was installed? (Rabbi M. Levin, Kansas City, Missouri)

ANSWER: This entire matter is governed by a simple biblical statement, "When you sell property to your neighbor, or buy anything from your neighbor, you shall not wrong one another" (Lev. 25:14). This law has been further developed in the Talmud and later codes. Maimonides made the seller responsible for disclosure of any defect to the buyer (Hul. 94a; *Yad* Hil. Mekhirah 18.1; *Tur Shulhan Arukh Hoshen Mishpat* 227; *Shulhan Arukh Hoshen Mishpat* 227.6; *Sefer Hamitzvot* Lo Ta-aseh #250). There is disagreement over the possibility of waiving such liability. Maimonides felt it could not be waived *(Yad* Hil. Mekhirah 15.6). Asher ben Yehiel disagreed *(Tur Hoshen Mishpat* 232.7); the discussion on waiver of responsibility was continued in the later responsa.

Traditional texts discuss specific items in which defects have been discovered. One of the primary grounds for recovering the purchase price involves an item which may have a dual use and the buyer finds it not suitable for his purpose. This would be true of eggs, which may be eaten or hatched, seed which may be consumed or planted, an ox which may be used for plowing or slaughtered for food, etc. If the buyer did not inform the seller of his intended used then he has no recourse (B. B. 90a; *Yad* Hil. Mekhirah 16.2).

In these instances, and others like them, the seller had to provide a sum which made good on the defect, but the items purchased were not returned to him. However, if the defect was major and in a permanent item like a building, then the buyer generally had the right to return the building to the seller, though he might settle for payment of repair costs. For example, Asher ben Jehiel spoke of a building which had been severely damaged by vandals during the period of the sale. In that instance, the damage was repairable, and so the seller was responsible for payment of the repairs. However, if the damage had been more serious, and if the item could not have been restored to its original state, then the seller would have been forced to take it back (Asher b. Jehiel, *Responsa,* Section 96, #7; Joshua Falk to *Tur Hoshen Mishpat* 232.5; Joel Sirkes to *Tur Hoshen Mishpat* 232.4).

Each of these instances dealt with defects which were readily discernible and not latent as in the case of the asbestos. Furthermore, they dealt with defects which were discovered in a reasonable period of time, certainly before the item was heavily used. I have found no responsa which deal with a latent defect or cases in which damages and liability were claimed decades later.

The matter of damages is much more complex because it depends whether this situation is classified as *garmei* or *gerama*. *Garmei* implies liability and *gerama* does not. There is a considerable amount of discussion on these two terms without clear conclusions (B. K. 24b, 48b, 55b ff, 60a, 98b, 110a, 117b; B. B. 22b; *Tur Hoshen Mishpat* 232.21 and commentaries; *Shulhan Arukh Hoshen Mishpat* 232.20, 386.4 and commentaries). The general rule seems to be that the governing authorities impose damages when the public order makes it necessary or desirable. When the damages are indirect, can not be foreseen, and no public benefit is involved, then there is no liability (*Tur Hoshen Mishpat* 232.20; *Shulhan Arukh Hoshen Mishpat* 232.21). For a recent discussion of this, see Epstein, *Arukh Hashulhan Hoshen Mishpat*, Vol. 8, 386.1ff; M. Elon, Hamishpat Ha-Ivri, Vol. 1 (Jerusalem), pp. 173ff.

In each of the discussions cited above, the defect was found either immediately or after a reasonable length of time; it was apparent and not latent. That is not the case in the question which you asked.

We must, therefore, conclude that traditional Jewish law would not hold the seller responsible for defects of damages after a long period of time has elapsed, especially as the defect was latent and unknown to both buyer and seller at the time of the transaction.

The entire matter may also be considered under the general classification *dina d'malkhuta dina*, and as the courts of the United States have decided that the seller responsible in this matter and that it is for the public good, it would be permissible for the congregation on those grounds alone to bring a liability suit.

Freeing Hostages

Questions and Reform Jewish Answers (New York, 1992), #237

Walter Jacob

QUESTION: A man in my family has been taken as a hostage by bandits in South America. How far may the family and the community go in order to obtain his release? (Daniel Stern, New York, New York)

ANSWER: The discussion of hostages and their ransom is ancient; captivity as a hostage was considered a terrible fate. The talmudic discussion of a verse in Jeremiah came to this conclusion as captivity was the last of a list of horrors (Jer 15.2; B B 8a). The later tradition elaborated further, and Maimonides warned that numerous commandments were violated by anyone who ignored the plight of hostages or even slightly delayed their redemption (*Had* Hil. Matnot Aniyim 8.10; *Shulhan Arukh* Yoreh Deah 352). Among charitable obligations, the redemption of hostages was primary; it took precedence over feeding the poor or building a synagogue, and funds to be expended for this purpose could be moved from any other obligation (B B 8b). Even the sale of a Torah was permitted for the redemption of captives (*Seder Hahinukh* #613).

The primary obligation rested on the immediate family, yet the obligation was also communal. However, matters were slightly different if the redemption posed a danger to the community. So, for example, Meir of Rothenburg refused to allow himself to be redeemed as that would have impoverished the community and set a precedent for taking communal leaders hostage. He, therefore, died in captivity (H. Graetz, *Geschichte der Juden*, Vol.7 pp. 203 ff. 476 ff.).

The redemption of a hostage is a major *mitzvah*; all the members of the family and their friends should participate in it. In this instance, the community may also be appropriately involved. Your description indicates that the man was taken hostage by bandits; this act does not have broader political implications as, for example, the taking of hostages by the Palestinian Liberation Front. Such efforts at blackmail of Western governments or Israel must be resisted and rejected. There the community may be hurt by ransom efforts, and that is akin to the problem which Meir of Rothenburg faced. Here, however, everything within reason should be done by the family and the community to obtain the release of the hostage.

❖ ❖ ❖

Jewish Lawyers and Terrorists

Questions and Reform Jewish Answers (New York, 1992), #238

Walter Jacob

QUESTION: According to Jewish tradition, is a Jewish lawyer obliged to defend Arab terrorists who attempt to kill Jews in Israel if the lawyer is designated to defend them? Is a Jewish lawyer obliged to defend terrorists who attempt to kill people in general if the lawyer is designated to defend them? Is a Jewish lawyer obliged to defend a member of the American Nazi Party when the lawyer knows that the goal of the American Nazi Party is detrimental to the Jewish people? (Rabbi Jack Segal, Houston Texas)

ANSWER: We should begin by making it clear that the current system of appointing a lawyer or the hiring of a lawyer to defend appears late in our tradition. Although a person might have engaged someone to speak for him, this was usually not an individual who made his livelihood as an attorney. A representative akin to the modern attorney was used if the individual could not appear personally due to illness or distance or if one of the parties felt inadequate to the test of presenting a case. Most cases proceeded without an attorney. The traditional Jewish court procedure saw judges engaged in interrogation and so they did much of what attorneys do in the American courts. Various responsa mentioned attorneys and dealt with problems associated with them but not with our problem (Jacob ben Judah Weil *Responsa;* Meir of Rothenburg *Responsa;* Isaac ben Sheshet *Responsa* #235; Moses Isserles *Responsa* and others).

Although there is nothing like a court-appointed attorney in the traditional system of Jewish law, nevertheless, the tradition may provide some guidance for Jewish attorneys in the United States and in the State of Israel in which the courts function differently. In these systems, an accused individual engages an attorney or has an attorney appointed. What is the duty of a Jewish attorney under those circumstances?

In order to answer this question, we must ask ourselves about the purpose of a trial. Our concern is justice and that was expressed by the Bible, which demanded close cross examination of the witnesses (Deut 13.15), as the accused was perceived innocent until proven guilty. The accused must be present during the examination of each of the witnesses who are testifying against her or him *(Yad Hil.* Edut 4.1). Furthermore, the defendant must be personally warned by those who saw the crime or by someone else (San 30a; Git 33b; Kid 26b and Codes). The examination must concentrate on precise facts and not wander afield (San 32b; *Yad* Hil. Edut 18.2; 22:1 ff; *Shulhan Arukh Hoshen Mishpat* 15.3; *Responsa Rivash #266).*

There are strict rules against self-incrimination and no evidence of that kind is permissible (Ex 23.1; San 9b; Yeb 25; San 6.2; 18.6 and commentaries). The defendant may plead on her or his own behalf in front of the court before the court begins its deliberations (M San 5.4), but is not permitted to say anything which might prejudice the court against him or her (San 9.4). If the defendant is not capable of speaking for himself, then a judge may do so for him (San 29a). If the matter involves a death sentence, then the court remains in session until the individual has been executed so that if any new evidence appears, the execution may be halted (M San 6.1; San 43a and *Yad* Hil. San 13.1 95).

This is merely a sample of judicial safeguards against injustice. It demonstrates the great care given to the defense of the accused and the efforts made on his behalf by the ancient system of courts. Lawyers or other representatives have not been involved, but the spirit of the law demands that we seek justice. We, in many modern lands, do so through an adversarial procedure.

The spirit of traditional legislation would indicate that lawyers in our system must participate in this effort to seek justice. This would apply to war criminals, terrorists, or others who may be tried in the United States or in the State of Israel. Jewish attorneys should consider themselves within the framework of tradition if they are appointed to such tasks or wish to volunteer for them. No one can, of course, be forced into such a position against their will. Attorneys help to assure that justice is done and that the accused has a reasonable opportunity to defend herself/himself within the framework of our judicial system. "Justice, justice, shall you pursue" (Deut 16.20) or "in righteousness shall you judge your neighbor" (Lev 19.15) will continue to be our guide.

❖ ❖ ❖

Punishment of Minors

Contemporary American Reform Responsa (New York, 1987), #3

Walter Jacob

QUESTION: What is the status of the minor in Jewish law regarding punishment for serious offenses? (S. Levin, Pittsburgh, Pennsylvania)

ANSWER: It is clear from a wide variety of statements that the father is completely responsible for the acts of his minor children. So minors would not be punished no matter what their crime, but the father would face whatever monetary penalty is appropriate (M. K. 8.4; Yeb. 99b; Hag. 2b; Git. 23a; B. M. 10b; *Tur* and *Shulhan Arukh Hoshen Mishpat* 182.1, 348.81, 235.19).

In a similar vein, the father is compensated for any injury to his minor children, including any humiliation sustained by them (B. K. 86b). The value lost was figured as if they could still be sold into slavery, as was possible in an earlier period (B. K. 97b).

In the case of the seduction of minor females, the fine went to the father (Deut. 22.28). If the culprit married her, he paid no fine (Ex. 20.15). In case of rape, he had to pay a fine, marry her and could never divorce her (Deut. 22.28). The Talmud increased the fine and included psychological damage (Ket. 29a).

Individuals above the age of maturity (12 for girls and 13 for boys) are considered responsible and may be punished as adults, but no capital punishment is permitted until the age of twenty *(Yad* Hil. Genevah 1.10).

If damage to property occurs due to the action of a minor, liability is incurred only if proper precautions have been taken by the owner (B. K. 29a, 55bff; *Tur* and *Shulhan Arukh Hoshen Mishpat* 421).

❖ ❖ ❖

Memorializing a Known Criminal

Contemporary American Reform Responsa (New York, 1987), #146

Walter Jacob

QUESTION: A man has approached the synagogue with the wish to provide a fund. Through it he would like to remember his deceased brother, who died in prison as a convicted felon. Is it permissible to place a plaque bearing this name or to name a fund after him? (F. S., Chicago, Illinois)

ANSWER: The entire matter of memorial plaques has a dual history. On one hand, we have wished from the talmudic time onward to encourage gifts, yet we have tried to discourage boasts about such donations. The medieval Spanish scholar Solomon ben Adret *(Responsa* #582) stated that it would be appropriate to list the name of the donor for two reasons and the *Shulhan* Arukh (Yoreh Deah 249.13) agreed: a) in order to recall the specific wishes of the donor so that the funds would not be diverted to another use; and b) to encourage other donors through the good example of that individual.

The question of donations from people of doubtful reputation or those having a criminal record has also arisen a number of times. It was always felt that such gifts should be accepted, especially as it is a *mitzvah* to support a synagogue and it would be a sin to hinder its performance. There were objections to temple sacrifices by criminals, but these objections were not transferred to the synagogue (*Toldot Adam V'Havah*, Havah 23.1: Shulhan Arukh Orah Hayim 152.31 and commentaries). However, there was an equally strong feeling that individuals of dubious reputation should not be honored; *marit ayin* and the honor of the synagogue are involved here.

It is, therefore, clear that although there is a strong tradition for memorializing the deceased through plaques, we should not mention a convicted felon by name. We might affix a plaque which read, "Given by in memory of his dear brother," without the specific name. We should not go further than this.

❖   ❖   ❖

Garnisheeing Wages

Contemporary Reform Responsa (Cincinnati, 1974), #57

Solomon B. Freehof

QUESTION: If the court orders the wages due to an employee to be garnisheed, and the employer is Jewish, has the employer the moral and religious duty to resist the court order, since the Bible prohibits withholding the wages of an employee? (Asked by Rabbi Joshua 0. Haberman, Washington, D.C.)

ANSWER: The Bible is specific in prohibiting the withholding of wages due to an employee (see Leviticus 19:13 and Deuteronomy 24:16). If, for example, the employee is a day-by-day laborer, he must be paid on the very day that his work is finished. This law is developed in full detail in the Talmud in *Baba Metzia* from 110b to

112b; and based upon the Talmud, the law is discussed fully by Maimonides in his *Yad*, in the laws of "hiring" *(S'hiros)*, Chapter 11. Then it is dealt with in the *Tur, Hoshen Mishpat* #339 and the same reference in the *Shulhan Arukh*.

There are certain circumstances under which even the strict Jewish law does not deem it a sin to withhold wages. According to some opinions, it is no sin to do so in the case of agricultural labor (evidently because the farmer himself gets his money only after the harvest. See the *Tur*.) Also, if the workingman knows beforehand that his employer has no money except on market-days, the employer is not liable for delay of payment till the market-day. Finally, the employer is never liable if the employee does not demand his wages. This is clearly stated in *Baba Metzia* 112a and in the *Tur* and in the *Shulhan Arukh* 339:10.

So it may well happen that the employee, whose wages are garnisheed by the law, may well appreciate the fact that his employer cannot violate the court order; and knowing that fact, he does not make the futile gesture of demanding his wages. Thus if he does not demand it (for whatever reason), the employer has committed no sin under Jewish law if he withholds the wages.

As to the moral principle involved, that may depend upon what sort of debt, for which the wages are being garnisheed. In the Commonwealth of Pennsylvania, for example, we have no garnisheeing of wages, except for the support of children and a wife (also for income tax). If it is to support children and wife, how could it be considered unethical for the employer to help in their support in this regard?

There is another ethical consideration involved. The sin denounced in Scripture actually involves two sins: a) the workman is deprived of what he has justly earned, and b) the employer dishonestly keeps (permanently or for a time) money belonging to the worker. But in the case of the garnisheeing of the wages to pay a debt (to a third party), while it is true that the workman is deprived of his just due, the employer at least does not have the use of the money withheld. It goes to satisfy the debt designated in the writ.

But actually the whole question is theoretical. The garnisheeing of the wages comes to the employer as a court order which he cannot fail to obey without legal penalty. The fact that he is compelled to obey the court order has special relevance in Jewish law. In all matters of civil law (such as these) the principle of *dina d'malkhuta dina* applies, "The law of the land is the law." In such cases it is the duty (the *Jewish* duty) of the employer to obey the law. This principle of *dina d'malkhuta dina* does not apply in ritual or spiritual matters. A decree to violate Jewish law in such matters should be resisted even to martyrdom. But the decrees of a secular court in *civil* matters are laws which (by Jewish law) we are bound to obey. Therefore the employer has no moral or *religious* right to pay the man his wages.

❖ ❖ ❖

Muggers and Money on Sabbath

Reform Responsa for Our Time (Cincinnati, 1977), #6

Solomon B. Freehof

QUESTION: An elderly Orthodox Jew, walking home from the synagogue on the Sabbath, was, of course, carrying no money. A hold-up man accosted him and, because the old man had no money to give him, shot and killed him. It was suggested that elderly Orthodox Jews, living in high-risk areas, should carry a token bill with them, say a ten-dollar bill, to hand over to the hold-up man and thus save their lives. Is there a liberal Jewish attitude applicable to this opinion? (Asked by Rabbi Reeve Brenner, Hebrew Center of Westchester, Tuckahoe, New York)

ANSWER: Non-Orthodox Jews do not hesitate to carry money on the Sabbath. Therefore there is no need for "a liberal Jewish posture" in this matter. The only type of permission to carry money that would be convincing to an Orthodox man would be that which is based firmly on Orthodox law. Let us, therefore, consider the strict halakhah on the question as to whether a man may carry money on the Sabbath if that act is likely to save his life in case he is held up.

First of all, there is no question that the carrying of money is forbidden on the Sabbath. (See Maimonides, *Yad, Shabbat 25:6* and *Orah Hayyim* 301:33.) The reason for the prohibition is not directly biblical but is based upon the rabbinical concept of *muktsa*. There are numerous types of *muktsa*. The one that applies here is the *muktsa* prohibition to handle such objects as are normally used to perform the type of work which is prohibited on the Sabbath. Since, therefore, it is prohibited to do business on the Sabbath, and money is considered to be specifically "set aside" *(muktsa)* as an instrument for doing business, money may not be handled or carried on the Sabbath.

However, it is to be noted that in this very matter of carrying money on the Sabbath, there are some grounds for leniency. Isserles, in his note to the law in the *Shulhan Arukh (Orah Hayyim* 301:33), says: "Many permit the carrying of money on the Sabbath if one is afraid that if he leaves the money in his lodging, his money will be stolen." There are some discussions in the commentators as to whether the money should be sewn in the garments or carried loose. But be that as it may, Isserles says: *Nohagin l'hokel*: ("It is customary to be lenient in this matter.").

Now, our problem here is primarily how to persuade the pious old man to carry the money for his safety's sake. One could well argue with him as follows: Since it is permitted to carry the money in order to save the money from being stolen, should it not be permitted to carry the money to save one's life from danger from injury or death? Of course, this is, in a way, the reverse of what Isserles permits. He permits the money to be carried on the Sabbath in order that it *not* be stolen, and we here would permit it to be carried on the Sabbath in order that it could be stolen. However, as we have said, danger to health or even life is more important than safeguarding the money.

Further discussion of this problem should also consider the laws of healing the sick on the Sabbath. If a person is dangerously sick, all Sabbath laws must be set aside completely. This applies not only to the secondary Sabbath laws like *muktsa*, the carrying of money, but also the strict biblical laws, such as lighting fires, etc. *(Yad, Shabbat* 2:1 and *Orah Hayyim* 328, 329). Furthermore, this violating of the Sabbath for the sick must not be done surreptitiously but openly by adults and men of standing *(Orah Hayyim* 328:12 based on *Yoma* 84b).

Yet actually there are provisions in the law much more relevant to our question than the fact that money may be carried to save it, or that a dangerously sick person may be saved by means which are in violation of Sabbath laws. The important and the direct law in this case is the law of *pikuah nefesh,* direct danger to life from accident, fire, violence. The law, as stated in the Talmud *(Yoma* 84b), and as codified in the *Shulhan Arukh* 329:1, 2, is clear and forthright. It is as follows: "All danger to life sets aside the Sabbath, and whoever is most active [in violating the Sabbath to save life], he is most praiseworthy." Mugging is clearly a source of danger to life, and if a life can be saved by carrying money, which is based only on the laws of *muktsa,* then certainly one is to be praised who can save a life by this violation.

Of course, it can be argued that we do not know whether the man might be mugged at all, or if mugged, whether or not the mugger would kill him. However, the law is also clear that when there is such danger of violence to life, we do not stop to count the probabilities. Thus, for example, if a wall falls, and if we think that someone is buried under it, but we really do not *know* whether or not a person is there under the ruins, though we suspect that he may be, or we do not know whether he is already dead or perhaps still alive, we must simply take for granted that there is danger of accidental death, and we dig into the ruined heap on the Sabbath *(Orah Hayyim 329:2).* This mugging situation is so frequent, especially in certain neighborhoods, that we may not stop to count the probabilities. We *assume* that the danger is present; and just as we are in duty bound to violate the Sabbath to save an endangered life, so the endangered person is equally in duty bound to save his own.

Maimonides, in his discussion of saving life on the Sabbath, cites the verse in Leviticus 18:5: "My statutes and ordinances which a man should do and live by" *(Yad, Shabbat* 2:3). To this he adds the talmudic amplification: "live by but not die by." This amplification of the biblical verse is derived from the Talmud *(Yoma* 85b) where, in the discussion of saving a man from danger, one scholar says: "Violate one Sabbath in his behalf that he may live to observe many Sabbaths." Clearly, then, it is a man's duty to save the lives of others regardless of whether the action involves violating the Sabbath. In fact, the law is that if we see a man attacked on the Sabbath, we may even prepare or use weapons to defend him, even if such actions are forbidden on the Sabbath *(Yad, Hil. Shabbat 2:24).* Obviously, too, just as a man is in duty bound to violate the Sabbath in order to save others, so a man is clearly in duty bound to save himself if he can. If, for example, a wall fell upon a person, we must, as mentioned above, remove the debris on the Sabbath to save him; so too, certainly, if the man is only half-covered by the debris and has the strength to struggle, he is in duty bound to remove rocks and stones and dirt (on the Sabbath) in order to save himself.

The old man and those like him are actually in duty bound to violate the Sabbath (by carrying money) or even to carry some repellent, such as mace or the like, if this is likely to save him, as the Talmud says, "to observe many Sabbaths."

❖   ❖   ❖

Collecting Synagogue Pledges through the Civil Courts

Recent Reform Responsa (Cincinnati, 1963), #44

Solomon B. Freehof

QUESTION: One of our congregations has used legal processes in collecting delinquent building pledges. Summonses have been issued to defaulting members, placing liens upon their property. Are there any precedents for this action? (From Rabbi Solomon K. Kaplan, Union of American Hebrew Congregations, Philadelphia, Pennsylvania)

ANSWER: The very fact that the question is asked reveals a feeling that it is wrong to bring Jewish religious disputes to the secular courts. Of course, it does happen in modern times that such matters have occasionally been brought to the courts in the United States, as, for example, disputes in Orthodox synagogues on the question of mixed seating, or questions of disinterment from Orthodox cemeteries. Nevertheless, whenever such lawsuits do come up, there is a general feeling in the Jewish community that the disputes should never have been brought to the courts—that to have done so was a *hillul ha-shem*.

This strong feeling against such actions is the product of a long tradition in Jewish law. The Talmud (b. Gittin 88b) denounces the resort to gentile courts. The *Takkanot* of the various medieval Jewish communities forbade Jews to resort to gentile courts. This tradition is recorded in vigorous language in the *Shulhan Arukh, Hoshen Mishpat* 26:1: "Whoever brings his case before the gentile courts is a wicked man, whose action amounts to blasphemy and violence against the Law of Moses, our teacher."

Of course that does not mean that Jews in the past never had recourse to the civil courts. There were circumstances when there was no other way to obtain their rights. If, for example, a debtor was influential and stubborn and refused to be sued in the Jewish courts, he could be sued in the civil courts (usually with the creditor getting express permission from the Jewish authorities). (*Hoshen Mishpat* 26: 2, 4, Isserles.) This procedure, as a last resort, is valid because gentile courts may (according to Jewish law) deal with matters of business debts. This limited validity is acknowledged by Jewish law because the "children of Noah" are understood to have been commanded to maintain courts dealing with civil law *(dinei mommonot).* (Cf. b. Gittin 9a-b.)

If the building pledges discussed in our question are to be considered merely as notes of debt, then, if there is no other way to collect them, it would be permissible to bring them to the civil courts for collection. But surely they are not precisely of the same nature as a business debt. They are rather what the law calls *sh'-tar matana,* a document of gift (*Hoshen Mishpat* 68:1). Jewish documents of gift cannot legally (in the eyes of Jewish law) be dealt with by the non-Jewish courts (*Hoshen Mishpat* 68:1).

In Jewish law itself, such pledges as certificates of gift are valid, legal documents. If, for example, Jewish law still had the executive authority which it possessed in past centuries, these pledges could be collected by force. The building pledges are equivalent to charity gifts, in general, and are deemed collectible even if the maker of the pledge changes his mind. The law is that the members of the Jewish community may compel each other to give charity *(kofin,* Yoreh Deah 256: 5).

To give *zedakah is* considered an inescapable religious obligation *(chova)* which even the poor must fulfill (Yoreh Deah 248:1). In fact, a promise made to give *zedakah* has the sacred status of a religious vow *(neder,* Yoreh Deah 257: 3) and, therefore, must be fulfilled without delay.

This serious concern with the legal validity of Jewish charity pledges is exclusively a matter of Jewish law. Non-Jewish law can have no relevance to it, unless we say that the pledges are also to be considered analogous to the taxes and imposts which the medieval community imposed upon its members *(missim v'arnunios)*. These, too, were collectible by compulsion. In fact, with regard to taxes and imposts, there are indications that occasionally, in some localities, the power of the civil government was called in to enforce payment. This resort to the "secular arm" seems to have been confined to Italy. Joseph Colon (Italy, fifteenth century) says *(Responsa #17)* that he sees nothing wrong in asking aid from the government in collecting the taxes imposed by the Jewish community upon its members. In fact, he adds, this has been the custom of many (Italian) communities.

Yet, after all, these taxes were to be paid over to the government, and the Jewish community would be endangered if they were not forthcoming It was understandable, then, that the Italian communities might, in desperation, call for secular aid in collecting them. But even in the case of taxes, there seems to be no evidence that the resort to government help was made by Jewish communities in other countries. Certainly this practice is not recorded in the general Codes.

The taxes and imposts were by their nature secular and civil. But a gift to the community for the building of a synagogue was a religious gift which was to remain within the Jewish community. Gentile authorities could not and would not be used to enforce an intra-community religious duty. There is only one exception to this, namely, the situation mentioned in the Mishnah (M. Gittin 9:8) in the case of a man ordered by the Jewish court to give his wife a divorce. If he refused this, gentiles might be asked to compel him to obey the mandate of the Jewish court. But even in that case the divorce is not a fully valid divorce (cf. *Tur* and *Perisha*, ad loc.).

Within the Jewish community, and in Jewish law, a pledge to the building of the synagogue is valid and enforceable. The same phrase used in the case of charity gifts is used for synagogue building gifts, namely: "The members of the community may compel each other ..." *(kofin zeh es zeh, Orah Hayyim* 150: 1). To enforce payment, the older communities used the power of excommunication *(herem).*

When the Russian government forbade the Jewish communities to employ the *herem,* then the phrase "to compel," used here in the *Shulhan Arukh*, seemed to reveal a violation of government decree. Therefore, in the *Shulchan Arukh* printed in Vilna, at the word "compel" there is an asterisk pointing to a footnote which reads, "by means of the government." This, of course, did not mean that the Jewish communities ever called on the Russian government to enforce this religious obligation. The footnote was added either by the censor, or else was added to disarm the censor, and to say that the community would not use the forbidden instrument of the *herem*.

It is clear, then, that, except for the time when Italian communities called for government aid in collecting taxes, the Jewish communities did not call upon secular courts to help them collect charitable or religious pledges. Jewish law considered that secular law could not validly deal with charitable pledges. And, in general, resort to gentile courts was held to be a sin.

The action of the congregation referred to, therefore, is contrary both to the letter and the spirit of Jewish legal tradition.

❖   ❖   ❖

Synagogue Contribution from a Criminal

Current Reform Responsa (Cincinnati, 1969), #14

Solomon B. Freehof

QUESTION: A man known or reputed to be a gangster wishes to make a contribution to the Temple. Should his gift be accepted? The question may also arise as to whether a plaque be put up in appreciation of his gift as is done with other generous donors. (From M.A.K.)

ANSWER: There is considerable discussion in the legal literature which relates to the question raised here. The chain of halakhic reasoning begins with the verse (in Deuteronomy 23:19): "Thou shalt not bring the hire of a harlot or the price of a dog into the house of the Lord thy God for any vow; for both these are an abomination ...." Aaron of Barcelona, in his *Safer ha-Chinuch,* explains the reason for the prohibition as follows: If a lamb is brought to the altar in the fulfillment of a vow, its purpose is to purify the heart, but if one brings a lamb which had been given as the hire of a harlot, it would bring back lascivious memories of the sin.

The law is carried over to the Mishnah *(Temura, VI, 2)* and thence to the Talmud *(Temura* 29a If., *Baba Kama* 65b). In the Talmud the application of the law is generally restricted. There are opinions given, that the word "harlot" used in the verse applies only to sexual relations with a married woman (which could not be legitimized by marriage). Other opinions say that only the object itself (e.g., the lamb) may not be given. But if the object is changed (if it be converted into money) or if corn be given to the harlot and the corn is converted into flour, or olives into oil, then these converted objects are no longer unfit and may be brought to the Temple in payment of a vow. So Maimonides records this as the Law *(Hilchoth Issurei Mizbeach, IV,* 14): "Only the object itself (i.e., the payment in its original form) is prohibited to be brought to the altar." The "hire of a harlot," etc., is the only "dirty money" mentioned in Scripture as prohibited as Temple gifts, and even these are restricted to the "hire" in its original form.

But there is a further and more important question involved here. The law as given in Bible and Talmud applies only to the Temple in Jerusalem and the altar, etc. Can it be legitimately extended to apply also to the synagogue?

There is considerable doubt about the justification of thus transferring and extending the old Temple restriction to the synagogue. The doubt is clearly expressed by the *Magen Avraham* (to *Orah Hayyim* 153:21). He says that the law refers only to the Temple, and that no classic decisor has extended it to apply to the synagogue except Jacob Well. (I could not find the passage he refers to in the *Responsa* of Jacob Weil.) Therefore the *Magen Avraham* decides that (since there is doubt whether the prohibition really applies to the synagogue at all) all questions on the matter should be decided *l'kula,* i.e., permissively.

Magen Avraham's comment is in reference to the note of Moses Isserles (ad loc.) who does apply the law to the synagogue, and says that no sacred synagogue object or *Sefer Torah* can come from "the hire of a harlot." But he adds that money (if the gift is con-

verted into money) may be used. As a matter of fact, the application of the Temple law to the synagogue was made before Isserles
(i.e., before the sixteenth century) by Rabbenu Yeruchem (of
Provence, fourteenth century). In his *Toldoth Adam V'Chava* (Section *Chavah*, Path 23, part 1), he says that "the hire," etc., may not
be used for a *Sefer Torah* or for synagogue lights, etc. But he also
says (in reference to Temple times) that if a man gave money and
she bought an animal, it would be permitted on the altar (because
she did not give the object that she received).

So as far as the law is concerned, it is clear that as long as the
man you refer to does not give the actual money (coins or gift)
which changed hands in the criminal transaction, it is not prohibited by the halakhah.

However, our present concern is not restricted to the letter of
the law, even though it does have weight with us. We are concerned also with the moral effect upon the community if we accept
such a gift. This is a delicate matter and must be carefully weighed.
In my judgment you *should* accept the gift, because it is his obligation (a *mitzvah*) to support the synagogue and we have no right to
prevent a sinner from performing a righteous act. For example, it is
a *mitzvah* incumbent upon a *Cohen* to bless the people (in the
duchan). But suppose a *Cohen* has committed a grievous sin, should
we allow him to bless the people? To which Maimonides says *(Hilchoth Tefilla XV, 6)* that he must perform the *mitzvah*. He says: "We
may not tell a man to add to his sin by neglecting a *mitzvah*."

So it is in this case. He, as a Jew, has the duty to support the
synagogue according to his means. We have no right to prevent
him from doing his duty.

But as to putting up a plaque honoring him, that should not
be done. Of course, in general, Jewish tradition favors recording
and publicizing the names of donors in order to encourage other
donors and also in order to prevent a specific gift-object being
used or melted down for another purpose. (See Isserles, *Yoreh
Yeah* 249:13, and the whole discussion in *Recent Reform Responsa*,
p. 203) Nevertheless, the putting up of a plaque would also be
honoring him as a person, and such a man is not one whom the
synagogue "delighteth to honor."

Yet even in this case, something constructive can be done. If
he wishes to honor his parents or some other close relative, a
plaque can be put up in their name and his name included as the

donor. In this case, besides giving a gift to the synagogue, he is honoring his parents, which makes it a double *mitzvah.*

To sum up, the money itself is changed from its original form and all authorities agree that it is acceptable. As for the donor, it is his duty to support the Temple according to his means and we have no right to prevent him from doing his duty. As for a plaque, he should not be so honored in his own right, but if he wishes to have a plaque put up in memory of a close relative, such a plaque should be put up, and his name mentioned on it as the donor.

❖   ❖   ❖

A Criminal as a Member of the Congregation

Questions and Reform Jewish Answers (New York, 1992), #41

Walter Jacob

QUESTION: A member of our congregation was (several years ago) convicted of brutally murdering his wife by repeatedly stabbing and drowning her in a bathtub in the presence of one of his children. He is serving a lengthy prison term and shows no remorse as he claims to have acted in self-defense. His children live with members of the congregation and attend our religious school. The man is still listed on the congregations membership roster. May we expel him from membership? (Los Altos California)

ANSWER: We must ask ourselves about the purpose of expulsion from a congregation, which is the equivalent of the *herem* or *nidui* in past ages. At times, the *herem* was invoked to protect the congregation or to indicate that certain kinds of action were considered reprehensible and would not be condoned by the community. This power was invoked for criminal acts, various types of dubious financial transactions, rebellion against the existing religious or governmental authorities both Jewish and gentile, or any person whose deeds seriously threatened the community. On other occasions the *herem* or *nidui* was used as a way of punishing an offender and forcing that individual to repent and return to the community. Maimonides listed the twenty-four possible causes for imposing various forms of the ban; they were casually mentioned in the *Talmud* (Ber 19a; *Yad* Hil. Talmud Torah 4.14; *Shulhan Arukh* Yoreh Deah 334.43). We should also note that in the last century the *herem* was used in unsuccessful attempts to quell liberal tendencies in various European communities. In other words, this was part of the struggle between Orthodoxy and Reform.

The various forms of exclusion, *nidui* and *herem,* were imposed for limited periods and seldom permanently. Furthermore, the bans remained in force only as long as the individual did not change his/her ways. The bans meant social and religious ostracism so no one could associate with the individual on a social basis or in business relationships. The individual could not be counted as part of the *minyan* or as part of *mezuman,* and his children were not circumcised or married *(Shulhan Arukh* Yoreh Deah 334.10 and Isserles). For most purposes he was treated as a non-Jew *(Shaarei Tzedeq 4.5).* He or she was also excluded from all congregational honors and privileges. As the punishment was so severe, some rabbis abstained from using it while others sought to limit its range (Solomon ben Aderet *Responsa V #238,* etc.). The *herem* did not necessarily preclude attendance at services or worshiping with the congregation although it often did. The authorities always hoped that the individual under the ban would repent, and this was considered as possible to the very end of life. Even convicted unrepentant murderers, who were executed, were buried in the Jewish cemetery albeit in a separate corner; they were considered a part of the community. Burial itself was considered an act of possible repentance; it was mandated in order to show proper respect for the human body *(Semahot* II; San 47a; *Yat* Hil. Avel 1.10; *Tur* Yoreh Deah *334; Shulhan Arukh* Yoreh Deah *333.3).* Apostates, who were frequently a thorn in the side of the Jewish community, were also still considered part of the community; they were permitted to be buried in Jewish cemeteries for two reasons: a) In order to spare the feelings of the surviving Jewish family members; and b) if they died suddenly, on the assumption that they had actually repented just before their death.

Clearly the community does not need to distance itself from this murderer in order to demonstrate abhorrence of his crime. We might, therefore, exclude this individual from membership in order to punish him, but it is doubtful whether this would be an effective tool. We might rather say that given the conditions of modern Jewish life in which a large percentage of individuals remains unaffiliated, we should encourage the affiliation of all Jews with the hope that those who are criminals or on the borderline of legality may be moved toward an ethical and moral life. We would make an exception only for individuals who represent a clear danger to the Jewish community (like Messianic Jews, certain political offenders, etc.). This particular individual can, of course, not attend synagogue services but the fact that he continues to be informed of congregational activities and receives the regular mailings may prompt him in a positive direction.

As an individual who is a criminal and has been convicted, he should be denied all special rights and privileges. He can not claim any of the honors or privileges normally accorded to a member of the congregation *(Shulhan Arukh* Orah Hayim 153.21 and commentaries; *Toldot Adam Vehavah 23.1).* This would include those privileges normally associated with his status as a father, he may, for example, be excluded from participation in any rites or services connected with his children. His name need not appear in the published directory of the congregation. As we normally exclude members who may be somewhat in arrears in dues payment, we may certainly exclude a member who has committed a serious offense.

This individual should be retained as a member of the congregation with the hope that he will ultimately repent and change his attitude. He may, however, be excluded from all privileges and honors normally due to members of the congregation.

An Unworthy Man Called to Torah

Current Reform Responsa (Cincinnati, 1969), #167

Solomon B. Freehof

QUESTION: At the regular Sabbath service, it is the custom of the congregation to call up two men to recite the blessings over the Torah reading. One Sabbath morning after the service, an officer of the congregation protested the fact that a certain man had been called up to the Torah that day. He said that the man (who was a lawyer) did not have a good reputation in his professional career. Is it justified to debar a man from being called up to the Torah because his character is open to question? Or is his reputation or character irrelevant to his being called to perform this religious function? (Prom C.G.B., Pittsburgh, Pennsylvania)

ANSWER: The question asked is of considerable importance because the answer given to it might well be applied to various other religious functions for which people are called up to the *bima*. The subject has been discussed sporadically in the literature. Simon ben Zemach Duran (fourteenth–fifteenth century, *Tashbetz* II:261) was asked whether unmarried youths may be prohibited from reading the *Torah*, either because the honor of the *Torah* requires only mature married adults to be called or because an unmarried youth could not remain clean-minded. He answered that according to the law, a young man is permitted to be called up to the *Torah*, and adds that even sinners are not forbidden to be called to the *Torah*; but, nevertheless, if the congregation, in order to make "a fence against evil," desires to forbid certain groups to come up, the congregation is always permitted to do.

Duran is cited in a recent volume of responsa, *Mispar HaSofer*, by Isaac Zvi Sofer (Jerusalem, 1961, Responsum 5) not with regard to the calling up of young unmarried men, but with regard to the more characteristically modern question as to whether a public violator of the Sabbath may be called up to the *Torah*. Sofer follows the decision of Duran, namely, that whatever be the actual rights of the individual in this matter, the congregation has, always, the right as a congregation to make decisions excluding sinners from being called up. He adds that many Hungarian congregations have long made such decisions as a "fence against evildoers."

The difficulties involved in this question are reflected in the very wording of the dispute as it was presented to Simon ben Zemach Duran. Some of the disputants considered that what was involved was *kevodei ha-Torah*, the honor due to the Torah, and therefore the dignity of the service. Other disputants insisted that to come up to the Torah reading was an obligation, a *mitzvah*, and therefore we have no right to keep a man from his religious duty.

The fact is that the legal literature never clearly defines the true status of this function. For example, is being called up to the Torah to be deemed as a religious duty, incumbent upon every Jew, just as praying three times a day is a duty? If it is a duty, then it would not be possible to debar a man from it, and thus prevent him from performing a *mitzvah*. Maimonides says *(Hilchot Tefilla, XV,* 6) in a somewhat analogous situation, speaking of a priest who had sinned: "We do not tell a man to add to his sin by neglecting a *mitzvah."*

But being called up to the Torah may not be a *mitzvah* at all. It may be a *right* that any Jew can claim and, therefore, could protest if he were not called up to the Torah after a long time. There is no doubt that many pious Jews consider this a right which they can demand, and object if they are not called up. The Talmud *(Berachos* 55a) says that if a man is given a Torah to read and does not read it, his life will be shortened. Therefore it is believed by some that to refuse to go up to the Torah shortens one's life (see *Yesodei Yeshurun* II, 201). A Yemenite, some time ago in Israel, sued the officers of his congregation on the ground that they were prejudiced against him and had not called him up to the Torah for a long time. He was suing for what he called his rights as a Jew. Certainly many Jews have that feeling, whether it is so in the law. Then again, it may be neither a duty on a man's part which he must fulfill, nor a right which he may demand, but a privilege which the congregation confers. In that case, the congregation can bestow that privilege upon whomever it deems worthy and withhold it from whomever it judges unworthy.

Since this basic definition of what the status of the ceremony is (duty, right, or privilege) has not been clarified in the law, the probabilities are that the status is vague and that it has the nature

of all three of these possible classifications. It is necessary, therefore, to see to what extent it partakes of each.

Is it a duty, a *mitzvah*, incumbent upon every Jew, to be called
up to the Torah? When a boy who is to be bar mitzvah is called up
to the Torah, his father is required to recite the blessing *(barukh
sh'petorani)*. Now, clearly in this case, this is a religious duty
incumbent upon the father. How could we possibly prevent him
from performing this *mitzvah*, even if he were a notorious sinner?
Yet, even in this case, it is to be observed that it is doubtful
whether the blessing is really required. The requirement is found
in a note by Isserles in *Orah Hayyim 225:1*, and even he is uncertain
about it and, therefore, suggests that in reciting the blessing, the
father should leave out God's name (a practice which is followed
in the case of all blessings of dubious validity, so that God's name
be not recited in vain). If, then, it is not, broadly speaking, a duty
to go up to the Torah, is it a right which a Jew can claim? To some
extent this may be so. Certainly a priest can count it as his right to
be called up to the Torah first. The law frequently discusses who
should be called up to the Torah, after the priest and the Levite
have been called up for the first two portions: a bridegroom in the
week of his marriage has precedence over a bar mitzvah; next, a
father whose child is circumcised that week; then a mourner, on
his *yahrzeit*. Are all these rights which a man can demand? The
most that can be said is that they have become customary rights.
The law does not make them firm rights, but a man can well be
aggrieved if he is denied them. If, for example, someone gives a
large sum of money for the privilege of being called up, the old
congregations would certainly call him up, and no one of the categories above would feel that they had a right to dispute.

Certainly the calling up partakes, also, of the nature of a
privilege because the congregation often calls up a man in order
to honor him. It will call up the rabbi for the third portion, which
is the first to which a non-priest or non-Levite can be called up.
That honor is certainly involved in the Torah reading is clear
from the statement in b. *Megilla* 23a, where it is said that while
women may be called up as one of the seven on the Sabbath, we
do not call up women because of "the dignity of the congregation" *(mipne kovodei ha-tzibur)*. Thus the dignity and the propriety
of the situation involved is a significant consideration.

It is possible to decide the matter more closely than merely
upon the vague fact that being called up to the Torah partakes

somewhat of the nature of all three, a duty, a right, or a privilege. Ephraim Margolies, the famous scholar of Brody (1762–1828), wrote a book dealing specifically with the questions involved in the reading of the Torah (*Sha'arei Ephraim*, many editions). In Section 1, paragraph 32, he discusses who should not be called up to the Torah. Most of this discussion is based chiefly upon two passages in the *Shulhan Arukh* which provide some material analogous to our problem. One in *Orah Hayyim* 128 deals with sinful priests and their rights to go up to bb# the people; and the other in *Yoreh Deah*, 334 (also *Orah Hayyim* 55:11) speaks of a man who has been put under ban, as to whether he may be included in the *minyan*, etc.

The implications of these two laws and their bearing on our question about calling an unworthy man up to the Torah have been rather fully explored in an interesting responsa sequence. It is found in *Shetei Helehem* (331) by Moses Hagiz, a Palestinian rabbi who lived in Leghorn and Amsterdam (1671–1750).

The incident which evoked this series of responsa throws some light on the social conditions of the time. In one of the Sephardic congregations, a man embezzled the money of the *chazan* and ran away with the *chazan's* wife. The guilty couple fled to Spain, but terrified by the Inquisition, they came to London. Meantime, the *chazan*, in poverty and anguish, died. The culprit in London was told by the *Chacham* to make a public confession of guilt. This he did in the synagogue, in the presence of the congregation. Thereafter he was frequently called up to the Torah. One Yom Kippur, the brother of the dead *chazan* was in London and saw this man holding the Torah at *Kol Nidre*. He bitterly protested. He said that this man had not returned the embezzled money or made any attempt to do so; his repentance is, therefore, insincere, and such a scoundrel should not be called up to the Torah.

Although this was a quarrel within the Sephardic community, many Ashkenazic scholars were consulted, as well as the rabbis of Mantua, etc., and among the Ashkenazim were the famous scholars, Jacob Reischer of Metz (*Shevut Jacob*) and Jacob Emden of Altona. Between them, they dealt with the implications of the references to the sinful priest in *Orah Hayyim* and the excommunicated man in *Yoreh Deah*. Most of the opinions were to the effect that since the man had made no attempt to restore what he had stolen, his repentance is incomplete and, therefore, he should not be called up to the Torah. This would indicate the feeling, at least on the part of most of the scholars, that a non-repentant sinner should not be called up to the Torah. This opinion is generally based on the *Orah Hayyim* statement that if a priest has committed certain crucial sins, such as marrying a divorced woman, wilfully defiling himself by contact with the dead, then if he is not repentant, he not permitted to bless the people. Two of the scholars, one anonymous and the other Jacob Emden, say that this is a bad analogy. A priest, if he repents, may bless the people because blessing the people is a *mitzvah*, a commandment imposed upon him ("Thus shall ye bless," Numbers 6:23). Thus it is clear in the minds of these scholars that being called up to the Torah is *not* a commandment before which we may not put obstacles.

As for the analogy with the law in *Yoreh Deah*, that a man who is under ban may not be counted to the *minyan*, Jacob Emden says that the law clearly states that only the man who has been officially put under ban is debarred. As long as a sinner has not been put officially under ban, he may still be counted to the *minyan*. This sinner in London has not been put under ban officially. Therefore he may still be counted to the *minyan*.

Jacob Emden then adds that being called up to the Torah is less important than being counted to the *minyan*. Women and children, although they may not be counted to the *minyan*, may, nevertheless (according to the Talmud, *Megilla* 23a) be called up to the Torah. So it is conceivable that this wicked man in London could be excluded from the *minyan* and yet be called up to the Torah. But Jacob Emden says that since he was not put under ban, and since, anyhow, being called up to the Torah is not as strict a matter as being counted to a *minyan*, then it might be a kindness to let him be called to the Torah. This might help him towards righteousness. Besides, he adds, we "must not close the door in the face of the would-be repentant." In fact, Ephraim Margolies in his handbook says that if it is not definitely proved that a man is a sinner, we ought to allow him to be called up.

Ephraim Margolies goes into specific details about who should not be called up. A man who is known to have taken bribes should not be called up to the passage dealing with justice and laws; and a man whose wife neglects the mikvah, etc., should not be called up to the passage which deals with these matters. On fast days, a man who is not fasting is not called up to the

Torah (*Shaare Ephraim* I, 17). The commentator, Shaarei Rahamim (Sabbetai Lifschitz) bases an explanation of these selective restrictions upon the *P'ri Megadim* (Joseph Teomim) to *Orah Hayyim* 141, end of paragraph 8, in which he indicates that such a man would be bearing false witness to the passage being read. But in spite of these selective restrictions, where there would be a shocking contrast between the reading from Scripture and the character of the man called up, Margolies concludes that, in the spirit of Jacob Emden: "If we call him up and some indignant worshiper scolds him, the embarrassment may lead the sinner to full repentance." The commentator Shaarei Rahamim to this passage in Margolies adds another leniency as follows: Although it is not permissible to call a blind man to the Torah, nevertheless we do call up blind people and illiterates because they do not read the Torah and we rely upon the reading by the official reader. Thus, he continues, we can call up sinners who should not be permitted to read the Torah themselves because nowadays we count on the reading by the official reader. (See also Jehiel Weinberg in *Seridei Esh*, II, as to Sabbath violators called to the Torah.)

We may therefore conclude as follows: While it is not clear in the law whether being called up is a duty, a right, or a privilege, the ceremony clearly partakes of each of these. A man of dubious reputation should not be called up for certain specific passages, where his character contradicts the reading. Nor, of course, should a notoriously evil man, such as the one mentioned by Moses Hagiz, be allowed to shame the congregation by being called up to the Torah. But in general, in less heinous offenses, as long as the man has not been excluded or ostracized by the community, we should not "shut the door in his face." We should always consider the honor of the congregation, yet be lenient and avoid complete exclusion.

CONTRIBUTORS

Richard A. Block is Executive Director of the World Union of Progressive Judaism. He has a law degree from Yale University and he is frequently published in the *Journal for Reform Judaism*, and the *Yale Law Journal*, and other periodicals.

Solomon B. Freehof (1893-1990) was rabbi of the Rodef Shalom Congregation, Pittsburgh, Pennsylvania; President of the Central Conference of American Rabbis and of the World Union for Progressive Judaism; and Chair of the Responsa Committee of the Central Conference of American Rabbis. Author of twenty six-books including eight volumes of responsa, *Responsa in Wartime* (1947), *Reform Jewish Practice* (1947, 1952), *The Responsa Literature* (1955), *A Treasury of Responsa* (1963), *Today's Reform Responsa* (1990).

Leonard Kravitz is Professor of Midrash and Homiletics at the Hebrew Union College—Jewish Institute of Religion in New York. He has served on the Medical Ethics Committee of the New York Federation of Philanthropies. Author of *The Esoteric Meaning of Maimonides' Guide for the Perplexed* (1988), *Commentary on the Ethics of the Fathers* (1992) with K. Olitzky.

Walter Jacob, Senior Scholar of Rodef Shalom Congregation, Pittsburgh, Pennsylvania is past President of the Central Conference of American Rabbis, past Chair of the Responsa Committee; and President of the Freehof Institute of Progressive *Halakhah* and of the Associated American Jewish Museums. Author and editor of twenty-three books, including *Contemporary*

American Reform Responsa (1987), *Liberal Judaism and Halakhah* (1988), *The Healing Past: Pharmaceuticals in the Biblical and Rabbinic World* (1993), *Not By Birth Alone, Conversion to Judaism* (1997).

Clifford E. Librach, rabbi of Temple Sinai in Sharon, Mass. has a law degree from New York University and clerked for Judge Robert E. Seiler, Supreme Court of Missouri. He has written for the *Journal of Reform Judaism*, the *Jewish Law Association Studies* as well as other periodicals.

Stephen M. Passamaneck is Professor of Rabbinic at the Hebrew Union College in Los Angeles and past Honorary President of the Jewish Law Association. He is author of numerous essays as well as *Insurance in Rabbinic Law* (1974), *Jewish Law and Life* (1977), *The Traditional Jewish Law of Sale* (1983) and, with others, *Introduction to the History and Sources of Jewish Law* (1996). He also serves as a Peace Officer in the Los Angeles Sherriff's Department.

Moshe Zemer is Director of the Freehof Institute of Progressive *Halakhah*. He is a founder of the Movement for Progressive Judaism in Israel and founding rabbi of the Kedem Synagogue-Bet Daniel, Tel Aviv. He is *Av Bet Din* of the Israel Council of Progressive Rabbis and Senior Lecturer in Rabbinic at Hebrew Union College, Jerusalem, he has also contributed numerous articles on halakhah in the Israeli press and scientific journals, and is the author of *The Sane Halakhah* [Hebrew], (1993).